FTERMATH OF EMPIRE

nith College Studies in History XLVII

Smith College Studies in History Vol. XLVII

Smith College Studies in History Vol. XLVII

AFTERMATH
OF EMPIRE

In honor of
Professor Max Salvadori

Northampton, Massachusetts

© 1975 SMITH COLLEGE STUDIES IN HISTORY
LIBRARY OF CONGRESS CATALOG CARD NUMBER (75–1728)

The Smith College Studies in History are published at irregular
intervals and may be ordered from: Order Department, Smith
College Library, Northampton, Massachusetts 01060

TABLE OF CONTENTS

INTRODUCTION

Hᴏ ɪsᴛᴏʀʏ is not made of events and dates. But as the years come and go, dates and events are woven into the fabric of history, to give it richness and meaning. The variety of history can be as sharply focused as the single fateful hour of a day and as sweeping as the span of a century.

1975 is the Centennial Year for Smith College. It is also the sixtieth anniversary of the *Smith College Studies in History*. The present number of the *Studies* is to celebrate both these events. It is also to remind us once again that a college is a living organism, a community of scholars teaching or learning, a community constantly renewing itself, yet keeping hold on its own past. Through Alumnae, Faculty and students the past, the present and the future always merge into one. Each year, at Commencement time, an Alumnae College brings back to the campus those who return to their past, which is also part of their present. It may be an excursion into the never-never land of Nostalgia. It is also a moment of intellectual renewal when students of the past reacquaint themselves with the resources of their college.

In 1973 the topic of the Alumnae College centered around the problem of Empire. In a world of disintegrating Empires and emerging nations new questions become acute.

7

What were the achievements of the great Empires of the past? What alternatives are there? What is the aftermath of Empire? To these problems Max Salvadori, of the Department of History, addressed himself throughout his teaching career, in his lectures and in his writings.

The Alumnae College of 1973 paid tribute to him in his year of retirement. The Centennial number of the *Smith College Studies in History* recreates here the program dedicated to a man who was a distinguished member of the Smith College Faculty for a quarter of a century.

Nelly S. Hoyt

EMPIRE LOST—MYTH AND REALITY IN
POST-IMPERIAL SOCIETIES: THE CASE
OF CENTRAL EUROPE SINCE 1918

EMPIRE LOST—MYTH AND REALITY IN POST-IMPERIAL SOCIETIES: THE CASE OF CENTRAL EUROPE SINCE 1918

EMPIRE LOST... Footnotes to Gibbon? Perhaps yes, perhaps no. Gibbon, you may remember, got his inspiration for the *Decline and Fall* when, at Rome on the 15th of October 1764, he sat amidst the ruins of the capital while the barefoot friars were singing vespers in the temple of Jupiter. There then was Gibbon's inspiration, ten centuries and more telescoped into one moment: Jupiter and the friars, Rome and the triumph of Christianity. And he set out to unfold that moment, in terms of the story of decay, at first as he thought merely of the city of Rome and then of the Empire.

Empires have their way of declining, as Gibbon exhaustively demonstrated. Yet as for Greece, was it not Horace who reminded us that "Greece conquered Greece, her conqueror subdued and Rome grew polished who till then was rude"? And as for Rome there was that *translatio imperii* which established the continuity between the Empire of Augustus and Constantine and that of Charlemagne and the Holy Roman Emperors. And, to extend that chain of dominion further, in 1860 Pope Pius IX in the liturgical Good Friday prayer included the Austrian Emperor, Francis Joseph, His Apostolic Majesty, in the place of the *Imperator*

11

Romanorum.[1] And even the parvenu Hohenzollern Emperor, the Kaiser, saw his Reich, popularly referred to as the Second Reich, in the succession of the first one, the Holy Roman Empire. What I mean to say, then, is that Gibbon's emphasis on decay does not quite fit my model. And I admit to a certain paradox, especially in a day and age when one is used to speaking of "Imperial Sunset," "Retreat from Empire," "Aftermath of Empire," "End of Empire,"[2] if I maintain that somehow "Empire" persists at least as a problem.

Perhaps as a skeptical historian with an overview of centuries, I might, when pressed, take the position that there will always be Empires and that that chain of dominion about which I spoke earlier will never really end because of man's quest for order, oneness, wholeness, power, glory. Or, to make my initial assumptions more modest, if less challenging, I might suggest that eagles and crescents cast enormous shadows which tend to assume a reality of their own even if the eagles have fallen and the crescents have set. Or, again, I might suggest that the British red on the map or for that matter the French green, the German brown which used to designate their Empires never quite fade. In short, I am struck by the survival quality of Empires.

Putting first things first I might briefly turn to the definition of "Empire" in Webster's Dictionary: "1. A group of

1. Taras von Borodajkewycz, "Die Kirche in Österreich," in Josef Nadler and Heinrich von Srbik, eds., *Österreich, Erbe und Sendung im deutschen Raum* (Salzburg, Leipzig, 1936), p. 311.
2. Max Beloff, *Imperial Sunset: Britain's Liberal Empire, 1897–1921* (New York, 1970); John Connell, "Retreat from Empire," manuscript referred to ibid., p. xii; John Grigg, "Aftermath of Empire: Britain and India since Independence," *Encounter,* XXXIX (June 1972), 8–15; John Strachey, *The End of Empire* (New York, Washington, 1959).

nations and states united under a single sovereign power, as the Empire of Alexander the Great. . . . A state characterized by having great extent of territory and variety of peoples united under one ruler, or by having emperor as the title of its ruler. 2. Imperial sovereignty or rule, . . . dominion. 3. An imperial domain; a domain under imperial rule."[3] The word itself, of course, goes back to the Romans, the Republican Romans. It defined the authority in the name of which the Roman magistrates wielded power abroad. This was the *Imperium populi Romani* which under Emperor Augustus was transformed into the *Imperium Romanum*. But Richard Koebner, the historian of Empire, reminds us that the "emotive significance of *imperium*," a matter of dignity and not abhorrence, was born on the Roman forum.[4] What this suggests is that Empire and imperialism, which is derived from Empire, are not necessarily odious and that the odious connotation in fact has taken hold of the concept only in recent times. Or might I say that there are types of Empires, and though I should like to avoid here the language of a child, however tempting, that would settle on good ones and bad ones, I must emphasize that there are different types: Empires by conquest and by consent; Empires in which higher civilizations hold sway over lower ones, and vice versa; maritime ones and continental ones; and so on. And I shall assume that there is in every case some relation between the type of Empire and the nature, the texture of the post-imperial situation.

Before I begin to discuss my particular case, Central Europe, however, I should like to comment further on the inadequacy of the definition. With Empire goes not merely

3. Webster's *New International Dictionary of the English Language*, 2d ed., unabridged (Springfield, Mass., 1947).

4. Richard Koebner, *Empire* (New York, 1965), p. 1.

the presumption of "great extent" of territories, indeed "universality" and exclusiveness, but also the presumption of eternity. I say "presumption" because history clearly does not bear out this fact. Still, the Roman Empire itself was believed to be destined for eternity, and to move into my bailiwick, Central Europe, the famous five vowel motto AEIOU which the fifteenth-century Habsburg Emperor Frederick III used widely on his documents and on his buildings to designate the aspirations of his House first meant *Austriae est imperare orbi universo* (Austria has dominion over the whole world), but subsequently *Austria est in orbe ultima* (Austria will be the last one in the world).

It is not sentimentality, not absurdity which makes me take this theme as my point of departure and hypothesis. The writer Franz Werfel found it hard to believe that universality should not be attended by eternity. "Is it true after all," he asked, "that what you are here calling a 'world' can actually fade away and die?"[5] This is the question that deserves investigation and an answer. Empires, and especially Empires like the Habsburg one, that have long been established and imposed an order, laws, a system of values, a whole set of habits and assumptions upon their world, may have a stubborn survival quality after all.

The problem of continuity, institutional and administrative, social and economic, in Central Europe has been elaborately treated by my fellow historians. But an Empire's survival quality is largely a matter of memories and images, of attitudes and desires, perhaps not so easily defined yet still discernable in the press, in the arts, in popular tradition and practices. This aspect of survival is my concern here. In what particular ways did it manifest itself? Were they all

5. Franz Werfel, "An Essay upon the Meaning of Imperial Austria," *Twilight of a World* (New York, 1937), p. 5.

14

residual, traditional? Or, were some of them new compensations for something lost? And if so, what kind of momentum did they have? These manifestations may be out of keeping with much of what we conventionally label the reality of a post-imperial scene. I would, however, argue that imagination and myth can assume a reality of their own and impinge on, indeed shape a society's history. It is in fact they above all that lend the aftermath of Empire the character of a period of twilight cunningly protracted, and make it a proper field of inquiry. And this period of twilight I am out to examine, in particular its cultural and psychological aspects, and finally to suggest at which point the historian can submit to the Shakespearian "The Sun of Rome is set. Our day is gone. Clouds, dews and dangers come; our deeds are done."

As you may have noticed from the gist of my remarks so far, we are deep in the heart of Central Europe, and this is not accidental. It may have something to do with my preoccupations and interests. But more: this is the area of the Habsburg Monarchy about which Karl Kraus, who has been rightly called the "first European satirist since Swift,"[6] quipped that it was a "laboratory for world decline" (*Versuchsstation für Weltuntergang*)[7] and of the Hohenzollern Monarchy during whose last years that hermit-eccentric Oswald Spengler composed the first volume of his pompous but compelling work *The Decline of the West*. Those two Empires were among the first to go as a result of the first World War, along with the Ottoman Empire, the chronic sick man of Europe, and, of course, the Russian one. They were pioneers in undergoing the trauma of dis-

6. Erich Heller, *The Disinherited Mind* (New York, 1959), p. 255.
7. Karl Kraus, "Franz Ferdinand und die Talente" (1914), *Untergang der Welt durch schwarze Magie* (Munich, 1960), p. 418.

solution and the loss of Empire, bigness, splendor—pioneers in living in a post-imperial world.

If *imperium* is nothing but power and Empires stood for nothing but subjugation, for order and peace imposed by force, our problem would be of a lesser order. We could deprogram, so to speak, the histories of Empires, whether of a predominantly political or of an economic nature. And in the one case, the political one, my task would be no more than to add to the already twice-told tale of the shock of defeat in 1918 and humiliation. In the other, the economic one, my task would be to explain why in spite of the Marxist-Leninist forecast imperialism in Central Europe was not after all the last stage of monopoly capitalism and did not give way to the much-heralded dictatorship of the proletariat.

The aftermath of Empire is, then, an area to which neither hard methods of history nor those of economics may at all do justice. Let me therefore, to suggest the nature of our problem, fall back on a literary document, a parable by Franz Kafka that might in all its elusiveness serve as a key to our problem. Its title is "An Imperial Message."[8]

The Emperor—so the story goes—has sent a message to you, the lone individual, the meanest of his subjects, the shadow that has fled before the imperial sun until it is microscopic in the remotest distance, just to you has the Emperor sent his message from his deathbed. He made the messenger kneel by his bed and whispered the message into his ear; he felt it to be so important that he made the man repeat it into his own ear. With a nod of the head he confirmed that the repetition was accurate. And then, before the whole retinue gathered to witness his death—all the walls blocking the view had broken down and on the wide high curve

8. Franz Kafka, "An Imperial Message," *Parables and Paradoxes* (New York, 1963), pp. 12f.

of the open stairway stand the notables of the empire in a circle—before them all he empowered the messenger to go. The messenger set out at once; a robust, and indefatigable man, thrusting out now one arm, now the other, he forces his way through the crowd; where he finds obstacles he points to the sign of the sun on his breast; he gets through easily, as no one else could. Yet the throng is so numerous; there is no end to their dwelling-places. If he only had a free field before him, how he would run, and soon enough you would hear the glorious tatoo of his fist on your door. But instead of that, how vain are his efforts; he is still forcing his way through the chambers of the innermost palace; he will never get to the end of them; and even if he did, he would be no better off; he would have to fight his way down the stairs; and even if he did that, he would be no better off; he would still have to get through the courtyards; and after the courtyards, the second outer palace enclosing the first; and more stairways and more courtyards; and still another palace; and so on for thousands of years; and if he finally did dash through the outermost gate—but that will never, never happen—he would still have the capital city before him, the centre of the world, overflowing with the dregs of humanity. No one can force a way through that, least of all with a message from a dead man. And yet you might receive that message as you sit by your window and drowse, while evening falls.

Franz Kafka, I should like to remind you, was himself the subject of an Empire, the Austro-Hungarian one; and the Prague Jews, one of whom he was, had all occasion, embattled as they were between Czechs and Germans, to look up to the Emperor as their protector. The Empire, in fact, was to them, of all its contingent groups, distinctly more than a mere political order, more than mere constraint. The Emperor had been historically, certainly since Joseph II had issued the Edict of Toleration in 1872, the protector. And Empire was to all of them somehow, as the monarchy had been to Shakespeare, part of a divine order. Kafka's fable

17

shows us the emotional significance of the idea of Empire and Emperor at its fullest and at the same time suggests the trauma of the aftermath. When Kafka writes "Emperor" he might mean God, or he might mean "The Emperor" (as he does in another parable); he might mean the "Emperor of Peking" (as he does in yet another parable),[9] or he might mean Francis Joseph.

I am not doing violence to Kafka then if I keep circling the orbit of both Central European Empires and I am certainly not taking undue historical license. The two Empires, Habsburg and Hohenzollern were, despite the differences between them, twin complexes. Offshoots, even though competing ones, of the same Holy Roman Empire, in a close alliance cemented by Bismarck, they were brought together again on that painful path which Kafka's messenger had to traverse with a message from a dead Emperor.

There is an inescapable mystique about the German word "Reich" which conjures up memories of the medieval Hohenstaufen Emperors, Frederick I Barbarossa and Frederick II the Sicilian, and the myth attached to both, born during the interregnum of the thirteenth century: that they were sitting under the mountain, the Kyffhäuser mountain in central Germany, with ravens circling above, eventually to grab the crown and the sceptre and to re-emerge and bring peace to the world. But of course the trouble with the German idea of Empire throughout its history has been that it is so ill-defined, so plagued by the disproportion between idea and reality. The very failure of 1848 to establish one Reich was a symptom of these tensions, of what the German historian Ludwig Dehio called that "lack of inner

9. Ibid., pp. 108f., 16ff.

harmony"[10] which had characterized the history of the Germanies from the time of the Hohenstaufens. Since Bismarck's days there have been two co-existing Empires, the Austrian one and the German one, each having its own sense of mission, of order, of dominion.

The imperial Austrian tradition was distinctly a supranational one. The Monarchy consisted of a multi-national area which had originally been the voluntary association of different historical units. And while the old—*tu felix Austria nube*—may no longer have meant much to the ethnically self-conscious nationalities of the nineteenth- and twentieth-century Monarchy, the associational, voluntaristic element in Habsburg empire-building, established by the marriage policy and repeatedly reinforced by the vote of the different Estates, remained a fundamental tradition in nineteenth-century Austria. Despite a record of occasional senseless centralization and oppression, even though Francis Joseph's *viribus unitis* often in effect was translated into a divide-and-rule policy over the various nationalities, the Habsburg Empire was ultimately immune to becoming, what it is occasionally called, a "prison of peoples." Its rationale throughout had been not conquest but order, its guiding ideal—indeed "mission"—not the imposition of one national culture upon others but a renunciation of national culture which Franz Werfel has called, in a somewhat sentimental fashion, the *sacrificium nationis* (the sacrifice of the idea and reality of national identity).[11]

As for the German sense of imperial mission it was newer

10. Ludwig Dehio, "Thoughts on Germany's Mission 1900–1918," *Germany and World Politics in the Twentieth Century* (New York, 1967), p. 107.

11. Werfel, "An Essay upon the Meaning of Imperial Austria," p. 13.

and more forced, more nakedly power-oriented than the Austrian, but also linked up with at least aspirations that transcended pure national interests. Even the Kaiser's German Reich had a sense of serving mankind, "fulfilling its mission to the world,"[12] if only to set itself up as a protector of free nations against French military or British naval hegemony—at least that is the way the Germans saw it—and to parade as liberator in the disguise of Hegel's World Spirit. A popular though second-rate German poet was inspired to proclaim: "One day the world will be restored to health by the German spirit" ("Am deutschen Wesen wird die Welt genesen").[13] These words were proudly and widely quoted in German lands. And German historians, philosophers, publicists, lawyers busied themselves to interpret the mission, as one of them put it, of "the German idea in the world."[14]

So Francis Joseph's Empire here, time-honored but distinctly ramshackle as Lloyd George put it, and the Kaiser's Empire there, new, brand new, indeed parvenu, both moved "shoulder to shoulder" to their nemesis, the war. Without going into the ins and outs of their last years, let me once again resort to symbolic foreshortening, and lean on a work of literature, that is, on Robert Musil's great novel *The Man without Qualities*[15] and its setting. Its theme is really the dusk of Empire in Central Europe, specifically that old K and K monarchy which Robert Musil playfully nicknamed "Kakania," and more than the dusk of Empire, the dusk of European civilization. Germany he called "a

12. Dehio, "Thoughts on Germany's Mission," p. 87.
13. Emmanuel Geibel.
14. Paul Rohrbach, *Der deutsche Gedanke in der Welt* (Düsseldorf, Leipzig, 1912).
15. Robert Musil, *Der Mann ohne Eigenschaften* (Hamburg, 1952).

20

paradigm of world history"[16] and Austria the "especially representative model of the modern world."[17] And there it is, the Collateral Campaign so-called, the "Parallelaktion," elaborately prepared by the Austrians to commemorate Francis Joseph's seventieth jubilee in 1918, but alas to match that of the Germans who had taken the initiative with their plans to celebrate the Kaiser's thirtieth jubilee during the same year. How easy the Germans' task was considering their Kaiser's snappy profile, self-confident if not arrogant, compared with the Austrians' in view of the fact that their old Emperor, "der alte Kaiser" as he was popularly called, that legendary old gentleman, was surrounded by doubts as to "whether he really existed at all."[18] In this case the planning for the festivity clearly was a tortuous affair, an incomparably tortuous one. Henry Wickham Steed, that shrewd Englishman, reported from Vienna about the paralysis of the "authorities," adjusting reality to appearances rather than appearances to reality, and about the abundance of talent "hypnotized by the general atmosphere of unreality."[19] The Austrians could not even settle on a motto that would do justice to the intent of the jubilee: "Back to Belief?" "Back to the Baroque?" "Back to the Gothic?" "Back to Nature?"[20] The fact was that the unsuccessful search for a motto merely accentuated the loss of a sense of "human unity embracing humanity's extremely varied activities,"[21] accentuated "the affliction from which mod-

16. Ibid., p. 1634.
17. Ibid., p. 1619.
18. Ibid., p. 85.
19. Henry Wickham Steed, *The Hapsburg Monarchy* (London, 1913), pp. 203, 205.
20. Musil, *Der Mann*, pp. 239f.
21. Ibid., p. 104.

21

ern man is well known to suffer and which is called civilization."[22]

Karl Kraus compared the critical situation of both Empires in his well-known quip that in Berlin everything was serious but not hopeless, but in Vienna everything was hopeless but not serious. But both, each in its own way, stumbled into disaster. One did so, one might say, through hubris, the other one through the paralysis of civilization. And what followed, in both Central European societies, was what Hugo von Hofmannsthal, the poet, called in a letter to a friend of his "the agony, the true agony of the thousand-year-old Holy Roman Empire of the German Nation."[23]

When Emperor Francis Joseph died late in November 1916, it had become clear to many that he, more than anything, had held the Empire together. The solemn, baroque, elaborate funeral cortege through the inner city of Vienna laid to rest not only His Imperial Majesty, but the Empire itself. And what followed, the short reign of Emperor Charles, Francis Joseph's great-nephew, was little but a postlude though not without dignity. Emperor Charles was a truly Christian man, a pacific man, uncommitted to the German alliance. But little was left for him but to see "his peoples" go, each in its way. He withdrew to a baroque hunting castle northeast of the capital and thence, under British escort, to Switzerland. And after two unsuccessful attempts to regain the crown of Hungary which, following a short Communist interlude, had again declared

22. Ibid., p. 105.
23. Hugo von Hofmannsthal to Eberhard von Bodenhausen, July 10, 1917, Hugo von Hofmannsthal, *Briefe der Freundschaft* (Düsseldorf, 1953), p. 235.

itself a monarchy, he was exiled to the faraway island of Madeira where he died a lonely death in 1922.

As for the Kaiser, he crossed the border to Holland in the early morning hours of November 10, 1918, not without having thoughts of some day triumphantly entering Berlin "at the head of my troops,"[24] as he liked to put it. But he stayed at the estate at Doorn in Holland, cutting down one tree after another, as was his hobby, until his death in 1941.

The loss of Empire in Central Europe was caused, as it normally is, by defeat. But its effect was, as is not necessarily the case, compounded by the loss of monarchy, by the disappearance of dynasties, long-established ones. And while humiliation was thus doubled by defeat, the sense of loss was aggravated in the setting of two rather hesitant revolutions, as were the ones Berlin and Vienna in 1918, by the change in the form of government from monarchy to republic. This complex shock in the Central European area due to defeat, loss of monarchy and loss of Empire found a parallel, if anywhere, in Russia, the Russia of Brest Litovsk, that disastrous treaty of March 1918 imposed upon Russia by the Central Powers, and in Turkey, which had ironically fought the first World War, the Ottoman Empire's last war in alliances with its traditional foes, the Habsburgs and of course the Hohenzollerns. But whereas Russia found its new legitimacy almost instantly through revolution and Turkey through Mustafa Kemal's (Atatürk's) resolute founding of a new Turkish Republic, the Germans of Central Europe were left humiliated, orphaned, deprived of their Kaiser idea, Reich idea, deprived and at the same time haunted by them, and once again abandoned to their own

24. Sigurd von Ilsemann, *Der Kaiser in Holland*, Harald von Koenigswald, ed. (Munich, 1967–1968), I, 31, 63.

disharmony, or as a French publicist put it in the 1920's, their "incertitudes."[25]

The new Central Europe, if it can be called such, had no legitimacy, no certainties. It is not hard to imagine that imperial messenger of Kafka's trying to make his way through these obstacles placed in the former capitals of Central Europe, Berlin, Vienna and perhaps also Budapest. The old palaces, mind you, were still standing and in fact in full prominence and the old street names would remain valid for a long time. But the *Schloss* in Berlin and the *Hofburg* in Vienna became empty shells. And yet there remained the *Königsplatz* (King's Square) in Berlin with the ostentatious Victory Column and that no less ostentatious *Siegesallee* (Victory Avenue) that led in a southerly direction to the *Victoriastrasse*. In Vienna all the streets spoke of imperial grandeur, even that not very elegant *Mariahilferstrasse* which had served Francis Joseph as the passageway between his two castles, *Schönbrunn* and the *Hofburg*. There remained the *Ring* around the inner city, which spoke, as it still does with all its adjoining monumental structures, of the Emperor's glory and his *via triumphalis*.

The mid-European community is "playing for its position in the world,"[26] so wrote Friedrich Naumann, the German publicist, a liberal imperialist, in his much discussed work, *Mitteleuropa*, that appeared in 1915 in the middle of the war and envisaged a democratic power structure, based on the two Central European Empires, in the heart of Europe. But not even this vision prevailed. Germany, through the Treaty of Versailles or the "Diktat," as the Germans irrespective of party affiliation preferred to

25. Pierre Viénot, *Incertitudes allemandes: La crise de la civilisation bourgeoise en Allemagne* (Paris, 1931).

26. Friedrich Naumann, *Central Europe* (New York, 1917), p. 180.

call it, had in fact ceased to be a world power. It still called itself a "Reich," indeed Hugo Preuss who was chiefly responsible for the drafting of the new constitution, the Weimar constitution, justified this carry-over as follows:

The word, the thought, the principle of "Reich" has for us such deeply rooted emotional values that I believe we cannot assume the responsibility of giving up this name. Tradition of centuries, the entire yearning of a divided German people for national unity are bound up with the name "Reich," and we would wound the feelings of wide circles without reason and to no purpose if we gave up this designation.[27]

Alas, his stance in no way reflected the actual position of Germany in the world. Neither did it reflect the image that the new Republic came to assume among the Germans.

As for Austria, it had become a non-power. It had even less legitimacy than did Germany. The "great fatherland,"[28] to which the historian Josef Redlich looked back from his "self-exile" in Cambridge, Massachusetts, was now broken up. Austria had lost its very identity. When Clemenceau said in 1919 that "Austria is what is left over," he was indeed correct. Austria was left a "land without name,"[29] as Karl Renner, the country's first post-war chancellor put it; a "state against its own will" (*Staat wider Willen*)[30] in the words of a nasty but accurate Nazi historian.

Among the various post-imperial societies I mentioned earlier, belonging to the period after the first World War,

27. Quoted in Koppel S. Pinson, *Modern Germany: Its History and Civilization* (New York, 1954), p. 402.
28. *Schicksalsjahre Österreichs 1908–1919: Das politische Tagebuch Josef Redlichs*, Fritz Fellner, ed. (Graz, Cologne, 1953), I, xi.
29. Karl Renner, "Austria, Key for War and Peace," *Foreign Affairs*, XXVI (July 1948), 595.
30. Reinhold Lorenz, *Der Staat wider Willen* (Berlin, 1940).

one should be able to discern, as I have indicated, certain models. The Ottoman Empire gave way to defiance on the part of the Turks, defiance at the Treaty of Sèvres, and then to the establishment of a modern Turkish Republic founded on the principles of nationalism, secularism and statism. The Russian Empire found a new legitimacy in Bolshevism which was a movement, as you remember, with a distinctly anti-imperial ethos—see Lenin's theory that imperialism is the highest phase of monopoly capitalism—but which has moved full circle from anti-Empire to Empire, that is, to a new form of imperialism—revolutionary of course, but also taking over many of the traditional geo-political aims and features of Tsarist imperialism.

In Central Europe it is almost impossible to talk in terms of a distinct model. Post-imperial Central Europe was adrift. To begin with, at least, all I can do is speak of moods. And what this may mean is that Central Europe in its moods represented a whole range, a whole spectrum of attitudes, and thus was indeed a workshop of the post-imperial mentality. Let me, by way of defining the spectrum, propose that at one end of it is the heroic mood and at the other end the civic, if not the philistine one. The heroic one in its many manifestations is and remains linked with the colorful imperial message, with a past splendid even though dead. It clings to bravado, to visions of grandeur, of the exalted, of something beyond the immediate and conventional. Meanwhile the philistine mood dwells precisely on the immediate and the obvious, forswearing extravagant aspirations to past grandeur. I hope you have noticed that I use both concepts, the heroic and the civic-philistine, in a purely normative and not evaluative sense. Both the heroic and the civic-philistine positions have their sublime as well as their ridiculous sides. While there may be dignity in the persistent vision of vast horizons, there is danger if they turn out to be a mirage after all and are pursued with passionate intensity. While in turn there may be folly in the ready surrender of imperial aspirations and grandeur, there is also strength and wisdom in the acceptance of a reality of smallness and insignificance and of striving to cope with them.

To give you some idea of the range of the spectrum, let me evoke some of the moods that it encompassed: the first revolutionary congresses of the workers' and soldiers' councils in Austria of 1919 called themselves, out of habit presumably, "Reichskonferenz."[31] And then, to shift the scene quite drastically, there is a letter by Paul Klee, a birthday greeting to his sister Mathilda of January 26, 1931: "When our old lord of hosts—now at Doorn—sat upon his throne, I was well off and I could never be in such a miserable plight as to be late with, say, birthday wishes for you. But now the times are a great deal worse. . . ."[32] And to shift the scene once again, now to the non-German world, to Split, formerly Spalato, that harbor town by the Adriatic: the time is the end of the twenties; an old ship, anchoring, flying the Yugoslav flag; an oldish officer, with sideburns à la Francis Joseph, coming down the gangplank and, interrogated about the origins of his ship, answering in that "Grenzerdeutsch," a kind of pidgin German that had customarily been spoken between the Balkans and the Adriatic, "yes, yes, that ship used to belong to us

31. Hans Hautmann, *Die Anfänge der linksradikalen Bewegung und der Kommunistischen Partei Deutschösterreichs 1916–1919* (Vienna, 1970), pp. 82, 90, 122.
32. Paul Klee to his sister Mathilda, January 26, 1931, Felix Klee, *Paul Klee* (New York, 1962), p. 67.

and then we took it over."[33] All residues from times past that found expression in a generation conditioned to think in terms of broad horizons. The German poet Gottfried Benn detected this kind of residual outlook during the second War in a former Austrian among his fellow German officers who seemed to have a "wider outlook," "perhaps," Benn conjectured, "because of the Adriatic and Balkan connections of old Austria."[34]

More recently a young Communist Czech man of letters, one of the leading men of the Prague spring of 1968, with no direct memories of Empire, spoke reproachfully of the founding father of his nation, Thomas Masaryk, because he helped destroy the unit that was Central Europe.[35]

I relate these occurrences, I hasten to add, as evidence, not as expressions of sentiment on my part. Yet sentiment, if not nostalgia did play a major role in the post-imperial mentality. Certainly the literature, the great literature of Austria after the war as represented by writers like Hofmannsthal, Musil, Werfel, to mention a few, was singularly preoccupied with the creation of what has been called a Habsburg myth.[36] On a less exalted, but all the more popular level, were film and operetta which enabled the public to revel in monarchic and imperial sentimentality. In the Germany of the 1920's and 30's, a whole series of *Fredericus* films went across the screens; "pure propaganda for the

33. Friedrich Torberg, "Ein sentimentales Vorwort," in Ernst Trost, *Das blieb vom Doppeladler: Auf den Spuren der versunkenen Donaumonarchie* (Vienna, Munich, 1966), p. 14.

34. Gottfried Benn, "IV. Block II, Zimmer 66" (1945), *Provoziertes Leben, Eine Auswahl aus den Prosaschriften* (Berlin, 1955), p. 159.

35. Ivan Sviták in a conversation with the author, winter 1969/1970.

36. Claudio Magris, *Der habsburgische Mythos in der österreichischen Literatur* (Salzburg, 1966).

restoration of the monarchy,"[37] commented Siegfried
Kracauer, the historian and critic of the German film. In
Vienna Fritz Kreissler's "Sissy" topped everything, the
story of the beautiful Bavarian princess Elizabeth being
wooed by young Francis Joseph, an operetta which had its
opening on December 23, 1932, and caused (we are told) a
"wave of general monarchist and Habsburg sentiment."[38]

In politics the obvious mood was defiance, which we find
in the positions and policies of the conservatives, reaction-
aries, or as they liked to call themselves in Austria, "legiti-
mists." Their story has not yet been fully explored. They
called themselves "Reichs" this, that and the other thing,
and even little Austria had its "Reich Association of
Austrians."

But the most dynamic force in post-imperial society was
not, after all, the specific nostalgia for a vanished Empire
and for a readily definable historical past. Thomas Mann
has reminded us that the defeated countries after the first
War were, by contrast to the victors who were still
sheltered by a sense of normalcy, conscious that the events
of 1918/1919 signified a divide of a much greater magni-
tude than a merely political one. The loss of Empire inten-
sified an awareness of cultural disintegration; it was felt to
be a symptom of the dissolution of religious and social
loyalties, of what Disraeli called "traditionary influences."
Given this malaise, what purpose would have been served
by a mere restoration of Habsburgs and Hohenzollerns?
Their Empires, it became evident, were irretrievably lost.
Post-imperial nostalgia was, then, mainly a harking after

37. Siegfried Kracauer, *From Caligari to Hitler: A Psychological History of the German Film* (Princeton, 1966), p. 115.
38. Bernard Grun, *Gold and Silver: The Life and Times of Franz
Lehár* (London, 1970), p. 245.

values rather than dynasties, and its sufferers invoked more and more a mythical past rather than an historical one.

It was Hugo von Hofmannsthal who gave expression to this sense of crisis of civilization in a striking and now famous address to the students of Munich in 1927. Lamenting the disappearance of certainties and the loss of what he liked to call "wholeness," he pointed to a "legion of seekers" throughout the country who were striving to re-establish faith and tradition, and whose aim was not freedom but allegiance, loyalties. It was in this connection that he launched the vision of a "conservative revolution," "on such a scale," he added, "as the history of Europe has never known."[39]

Now Hofmannsthal was variously warned at the time that the expression in this form of his idea had given support to doubtful elements.[40] After the first World War both Germany and Austria were virtually flooded with imperial visions by sundry "seekers," preachers and prophets. The two Republics, the German and the Austrian, both improvised ones and no more, were not regarded by their citizens otherwise than as interregna, manifestations of a "time without emperor, a dreadful time" ("die kaiserlose Zeit, die schreckliche Zeit").[41] And the further the reality of Empire receded into history, the more the void was filled by the construction of a new myth. In 1933 William Butler Yeats wrote a friend of his: "Served in India, is crippled

39. Hugo von Hofmannsthal, *Das Schrifttum als geistiger Raum der Nation* (Munich, 1927), p. 31.

40. Thomas Mann to Professor Karl Viëtor, December 4, 1946; Max Rychner to Hugo von Hofmannsthal, Zürich, November 10, 1927, *Süddeutsche Zeitung, Feuilleton*, September 29/30, 1973.

41. Immanuel Geiss, "Reich und Nation," *Aus Politik und Zeitgeschichte: Beilage zur Wochenzeitung Das Parlament* (Bonn), April 14, 1973, p. 17.

with wounds . . . and therefore dreams a heroic dream."[42]
Just this was the case in Central Europe. A whole generation of German and Austrian middle-class youth, most
visibly organized in the various groups of the Youth Movement, was gripped by a sense of spiritual homelessness and
despair over the hard realities of modern living and set itself
apart from state and society in search for some new Reich.
Above and beyond a lost past and a rejected present emerged
that dream, once again heroic—the Germans like to call it
"faustian"—that dream of that better Reich, whether it was
called the "Innere Reich," the "New Reich" (Stefan
George)[43] or the "Third Reich" (Moeller van den Bruck,
from whom Hitler took his own concept).[44]

Fascism itself is of course an integral part of the post-
imperial situation in Central Europe. Adolf Hitler himself,
the visionary of the Third Reich, who in 1938 brought
Austria and Germany together, I need hardly remind you,
was an Austrian by birth and a drifter in the imperial capital
during the early years of the century. He was a post-imperial
figure of a distinct type. There were many German-Aus-
trians who were unable and unwilling to cope with multi-
nationality, which was after all the basic condition of the
Habsburg Empire. Lord Acton has said that Christianity
rejoices in the mixture of races; Hitler did not: the old
Habsburg Empire was to him a "fruit salad of peoples,"[45]
as he put it, and it was precisely Hitler's inability to cope
with the actual problems of Empire, the real Empire, which

42. William Butler Yeats to Olivia Shakespear, July 23, 1933, *The
Letters of W. B. Yeats*, Allan Wade, ed. (New York, 1955), p. 813.
43. Stefan George, *Das neue Reich* (Berlin, 1928).
44. Arthur Moeller van den Bruck, *Das dritte Reich* (Berlin, 1923).
45. *Hitler's Secret Conversations 1941–1944*, H. R. Trevor-Roper,
ed. (New York, 1953), p. 191.

made him chase after the myth and mirage. Hitler's Reich then represented in fact the last fever in that agony of Empire in Central Europe.

If there was an underlying mood in German Fascism, cultural and political, it was the lament over the loss of wholeness, and the urge, as George Mosse rightly put it, to recapture the "whole man."[46] But it was here that danger lay, namely, in the attempt on the part of National Socialism to make a mythical Reich come true. The myth of an ideal past, in fact an imaginary past, could be realized only at the price of terror; alas, under the aegis of Fascism the "whole man" emerged not reconstructed but humiliated. The attempt to overcome an inevitable fragmentariness and to compensate for an irretrievably lost wholeness ended in barbarism.

To complete our projected spectrum, here is one final thought on the civic-philistine mood. If you probe deep enough in the history of Weimar Germany you will find that mood among the so-called "mediocrities" who lost out against the so-called "heroes,"[47] men like Friedrich Ebert. The Republic's first president and a moderate socialist, he tried hard, if unsuccessfully, to steer a course, however unglamorous, clear of a radicalization of the right which we know now tended to prolong the agony of Empire, and clear of that radicalism of the left which we know aided and abetted a new form of Empire.

And, to turn to Austria once again, the case of Ignaz Seipel is illustrative. One of Austria's leading statesmen of the era between the two Wars, churchman and member of

46. George L. Mosse, "The Genesis of Fascism," *Journal of Contemporary History*, I (no. 1, 1966), 15.

47. John Mander, *Great Britain or Little England?* (London, 1963), p. 203.

the last imperial cabinet of Emperor Charles, he was a transitional figure altogether between the imperial past and a future of coming to terms with smallness. His loyalties were clearly with the old Empire as well as with the Church. It has been said of him that he was "born too late" and that the new Austria was far too small for a man of his horizons, political genius and ambition. "To cultivate our own little garden and to show it to foreigners in order to make money out of it are no proper tasks for the inhabitants of the Carolingian *Ostmark* and the heirs of the conquerors of the Turks."[48]

Nevertheless he was a realist and found it a challenge to apply Metternichian statecraft and concepts to a power as insignificant as Austria had become after the breakup of the Monarchy. Time and again, in public and in private, he repeated his "Hic Rhodus, hic salta!," and he said that he loved the new state "because it is and because it could not be unless God after all wanted it."[49] Being a realist, he became the father of a *de facto* neutrality for little Austria, which became a *de lege* reality after the second World War.

The second World War acted in fact as the catharsis for the Reich idea in Central Europe. After the defeat of 1945 there were no more dreams, no more illusions about the Reich in Central Europe. Berlin is now divided, so is Germany, and neither half pretends to be a Reich. In Vienna, the magnificient *Heldenplatz* (Heroes' Square), with the equestrian monuments of Prince Eugene of Savoy and Archduke Charles, nowadays serves as a parking lot for the

48. Ignaz Seipel, letter to Dr. W. Bauer in Paul Sweet, "Seipel's Views on Anschluss in 1928: An Unpublished Exchange of Letters," *Journal of Modern History*, xix (December 1947), 323.
49. *Sten. Prot., 73. Sitzung d. Konst. Nationalversammlung*, April 20, 1920, 2122.

all too numerous cars of Austria's at last affluent society. This is the world, in short, of Conrad Adenauer and Willy Brandt and their Austrian counterparts Leopold Figl and Bruno Kreisky. And the imperial message, "as you sit by your window and drowse, while evening falls" has been, so it seems, relegated to us historians, rather than the politicians, to interpret.

In retrospect Karl Kraus's claim (Austria as a "laboratory for world decline") and Musil's (Germany as "a paradigm of world history" and Austria as an "especially representative model of the modern world") are borne out only in a very qualified way. No doubt the End of Empire, by now a general European phenomenon, made itself felt in Central Europe before it did so in the Western European societies. But there, in Central Europe, the loss was accompanied by convulsions which were unique to the area. I have dealt, of course, chiefly with the German Central Europe rather than the non-German East Central Europe; in the "Germanies" the process of retrenchment was clearly plagued by two decisive facts. It coincided with a cultural malaise, with "anti-industrial yearnings" (Geoffrey Barraclough) from which England certainly had recovered since the days of Matthew Arnold and Ruskin. Hence the ascendency, in the 1920's and 30's in Central Europe, of myth over reality. And the successors to Empire had no natural German national area to fall back on, no clearly defined home territory, no distinct nationhood. The result was uncertitude all over, a post-imperial expansionism, so to speak, of which the Anschluss of March 1938 was but the first step. And the coincidence of the cultural and the national malaise in the period after the first World War was intricately tied to the phenomenon of National Socialism.

The convulsions that seized East Central Europe between the wars, that made Woodrow Wilson's "New Europe" so-called stumble from one crisis to another, and that made most successor states of the Habsburg Monarchy succumb to some form of autocracy, dictatorship, native or imitative Fascism, and eventually to Nazi control, these convulsions were by no means conquered when the fate of the second World War brought that area under the sway of the "new imperialism" of Soviet Russia. Of course one country in East Central Europe, Yugoslavia, that had disentangled itself from what Rebecca West called in her grand post-imperial epic *Black Lamb and Grey Falcon* "that unnecessary monarchy," has been able to keep aloof from the Soviet bloc; and a sweet irony of history would have it that its ruler, Marshall Tito, in his role of presiding over and controlling his multi-national realm has frequently been spoken of as "the last of the Habsburgs."

For Western Europe the Central European model is applicable, but in a limited way, that is, in relation to certain moods. But while the temptation of Fascism, be it in the form of the *Camelots du Roi* or of the "paras" or of Sir Oswald Mosley, was there, Fascism did not become a clear and present danger in Western Europe between the wars and after the second one. Might I just parenthetically suggest that one distinct aspect of the Munich agreement of September 1938 was, as far as Britain and Germany were concerned, that it was thought of as a salvage operation for Empires: the British Empire and a revived one in Central Europe. Suffice it to say here that Western Europe has escaped many of the pains that accompanied the aftermath of Empire in Central Europe. And if philistinism is considered an inevitable mark of a post-imperial society, let me take comfort from Robert Musil who remarked almost half a century ago:

The expenditure of muscular energy made by a citizen quietly going about his business all day long is considerably greater than that of an athlete who lifts huge weights once a day. Physiologically this has been established, and so doubtless the sum-total of little everyday exertions . . . does bring far more energy into the world than the deeds of heroes; indeed, the heroic exertion appears positively minute, like a grain of sand laid, in some act of illusiory immensity, upon a mountain top. . . .[50]

Klemens von Klemperer

50. Musil, *Der Mann*, pp. 12f.

THE OTTOMAN EMPIRE IN THE CONTEMPORARY MIDDLE EAST

THE OTTOMAN EMPIRE IN THE
CONTEMPORARY MIDDLE EAST

W HAT I should like to do this morning is to focus upon one particular institution of the great age of the Ottoman Empire: the so-called *millet* system, that system of communal self-government (communal in the religious sense) by which the Ottoman state governed its subjects.[1] I should like to speak as well of the destruction of the *millet* system under the onslaught of the West and, finally, of what may be the relevance of that broken institution for the contemporary Middle East, more specifically that area known as the Fertile Crescent—an area which today embraces the states of Syria, Lebanon, Jordan, Israel and Iraq. Let me provide, in the form of three quotations, anchors for my tripartite discussion. You will note that not one of them is drawn from the majority element in the Ottoman Empire; I mean of course the Muslims. I take it as obvious that for one interested in the condition of a society it is wiser to look to the marginal communities first, for they are an almost unfailing index to the health and temper of that society. Strains usually manifest themselves first on the periphery.

The first quotation I would impart is drawn from a

1. The Turkish term *millet*, from the Arabic *millah*, denotes "religious community."

chronicle written in the mid-seventeenth century by an Arab Christian, the Archdeacon Paul, in the course of a journey he and his father undertook to what he termed "the land of the Christians"—that is, the Danubian principalities and Holy Russia. The archdeacon meant of course "the land of the *Orthodox* Christians," for his father and travelling companion was no other than the Orthodox Christian Patriarch of Antioch. On their journey these two Arab Christian Ottoman subjects were witness to atrocities but recently visited upon some Russian Orthodox by the Catholic Poles. The scene elicited these comments from the Archdeacon Paul:

We all wept much over the thousands of martyrs who were killed by these impious wretches, the enemies of the faith. . . . O you infidels! O you monsters of impurity! O you hearts of stone! What had the nuns and women done? What the girls and boys and infant children, that you should murder them? . . . And why do I pronounce [the Poles] accursed? Because they have shown themselves more debased and wicked than the corrupt worshippers of idols, by their cruel treatment of Christians, thinking to abolish the very name of Orthodox. God perpetuate the empire of the Turks for ever and ever! For they take their impost, and enter into no account of religion, be their subjects Christians or Nazarenes, Jews or Samarians.[2]

Such, around 1650, was probably the representative attitude of the Ottoman Christian toward the Muslim *imperium* to which he was subject.

A half-century later the weather had apparently turned, for we read in a letter written in 1706 by an Arab Christian archbishop to Louis XIV these words:

2. This translation of the original Arabic derives from: Paul of Aleppo, *The Travels of Macarius*, trans. F. C. Belfour, I (2 vols.; London, 1836), 165.

Though our necks be bent under the yoke of the Muslims, we regard ourselves only as your subjects.[3]

If the archbishop's altered allegiance was not shared by most Ottoman Christians, his appeal to the extra-Ottoman authority—be it French, English, Russian or Papal—would become typical of the Sultan's non-Muslim subjects before the eighteenth century expired.

The third and final quotation I draw, as it were, from yesterday, from an essay written twenty years ago by a certain Elie Kedourie, a displaced Jew of an old Baghdadi family, now teaching at the London School of Economics. Kedourie, in 1952 already persuaded of the unlikelihood that the post-Ottoman Middle East would, on the basis of the nation-state develop viable societies, remarked in a manner curiously reminiscent of the Archdeacon Paul three centuries earlier:

The measure of the failure is that today the west should be exhorted to build in the east nations where 'Moslems, Christians and Jews can and will live in harmony.' The Ottoman state was organized in such a way as to fulfil precisely this requirement.[4]

*   *   *

The Archdeacon Paul wrote on the eve of the transformation of the Ottoman world, at a time when the characteristic institutions of the Ottoman Empire could still be seen functioning with something like integrity. The century which followed the archdeacon's panegyric to the Ottoman *imperium* witnessed the gradual shift in the balance of

3. This translation of the original Arabic derives from: Robert M. Haddad, *Syrian Christians in Muslim Society: An Interpretation* (Princeton, 1970), p. 56.

4. Elie Kedourie, *The Chatham House Version and Other Middle-Eastern Studies* (New York, 1970), pp. 315–316.

power in southeastern Europe, central Asia and the Middle East from Islam to Christendom. We shall remark the consequences of that shift but first we ought to note those institutions which, inspiring the Arab archdeacon's admiration around 1650, may yet have relevance to the contemporary Middle East.

The Ottoman Empire was at once Islamic and multi-ethnic, multi-linguistic and multi-religious. An analogy to its historic antagonist, the Habsburg Empire—itself multi-ethnic, multi-linguistic, multi-religious but Christian—may be useful so long as one bears in mind that the religious diversity of the Empire of the Habsburgs was much less pronounced than that which characterized the Ottoman Empire and today characterizes several of its successor states. The Ottoman Empire was Islamic in the sense that full "citizenship" presupposed adherence to orthodox (Sunni) Islam, that its rulers were orthodox Muslims and that political legitimacy was, in theory and almost always in practice, associated with the ruler's ability both to defend and push forward the frontiers of "The Abode of Islam" and to uphold the Divine Law of Islam, Law to which the rulers themselves were subject. In these respects the Ottoman Empire differed little from its Islamic predecessors since the great Arab conquests of the seventh century. Nor in the fact of its ethnic, linguistic and religious heterogeneity may the Ottoman state be described as unique in the annals of Islam. For Islam, from its inception, had accorded to non-Muslims of *the* monotheistic tradition a special place. Jews and Christians were designated in the Qur'an itself (to Muslims the literal word of God) as People of the Book, that is, as people to whom God had vouchsafed legitimate revelations through legitimate prophets. They had, however, in their perversity, added to and detracted from these

42

revelations so that God, in His mercy, brought to Muhammad (the last, the seal of the prophets) the final, complete and perfect revelation, superseding those of the Jews and Christians and destined, through the hands of the newly chosen, to bring all humanity to submission (Islam) to the will of the One God.

But whatever the perversity of Jew and Christian it was ever clear that they were not to be confused with those who had never received God's word. For the pagan, Islamic theory (though almost never the practice) dictated a clean choice between Islam and the sword. Jews and Christians, on the other hand, were to be given the less traumatic choice between Islam and payment of a special tax. To those who would endure in error, spurning Islam in favor of the tax and the more or less free exercise of their ancestral faith, certain social and legal liabilities would adhere. Jews and Christians then were "second-class citizens" of the Islamic state but nonetheless "citizens," possessed of well-defined rights and obligations which found sanction not in the whim of rulers or the temper of the times but in the Law of God itself. And as "citizens" they were granted from earliest Islamic times wide communal autonomy under their own religious leaders who were themselves responsible to their Muslim governors. If, on one hand, the political and social subordination of Jews and Christians for over a millennium tended to deplete their numbers and creative resources, Islamic tolerance virtually ensured their communal survival. Islam's studied toleration of these "nations within the nation" must stand in happy contrast to historic Christendom's usual methods of dealing with non-Christians, not to mention heterodox Christians.

So when Turks, beginning in the late thirteenth century and led by the house of Osman (from whence "Ottoman"), won themselves an Empire which came to embrace the Christian Balkans and the Islamic Middle East they fell heir to the definitions I have just outlined, definitions which, in the Ottoman state, received concrete institutional expression in the *millet* system, that system by which the sundry non-Muslim subjects of the Sultans were governed. And the Archdeacon Paul's tribute to the "empire of the Turks" testifies to the decency with which Islam as well as the Turks usually discharged their Qur'anic obligations toward the People of the Book. Even in his posture toward Islamic heterodoxy—always a more exacting test of tolerance than the stance assumed before unambiguous infidelity—the sternly Sunni Ottoman Turk is not altogether to be despised.

But if this essential Islamic tolerance of diversity deserves emphasis, so too does the fact that any marginal community, any community of "second-class citizens," will, if provided an opportunity, strike out for independence or, should this prove impossible, will attempt to redefine to its own advantage that order which pronounces it marginal. Both tendencies were to be given free rein as the nationalist virus made its way eastward into the Ottoman Empire, first and with most clear-cut results in the Christian Balkans, later and with much less definitive results in the Islamic Middle East, still in the modern era Islamic but still, precisely because of the Islamic tolerance enshrined in the *millet* system, multi-ethnic, multi-linguistic and multi-religious. But this is to anticipate our story. First a few remarks about the consequences of that shift in the balance of power between Europe and the Ottoman Empire, which occurred between 1650 and 1750 and left this last great Islamic Empire utterly exposed to the depredations of those within and without who marched to the Western drum.

While the author of our second quotation, the Syrian

archbishop who in 1706 assured Louis XIV of his and his community's loyalty to The Eldest Daughter of the Church, was able, with that special acuteness of the marginal man, to discern where tomorrow's power lay, most Ottoman Muslims were able to cling for almost a century longer to their myth of military and cultural superiority to Christendom. Yet even before 1529 when the Turk stood for the first time before Vienna and all Europe trembled, his contempt for the Frank and all his works had been woefully out of date. Western Europe had in fact already embarked upon an expansion which would, in the course of the eighteenth and nineteenth centuries, bring virtually the entire world within the Western orbit. And in conjunction with this economic and political expansion came the new science and technology, the new ideologies and institutional arrangements, perhaps none of them more destructive of traditional non-Western societies than the concept of the nation-state. The West, often quite inadvertently, *defined* and for that became the envy and curse of the entire globe. To explain why the Muslim world, despite the richness of its own philosophic and scientific heritage, had neither brought forth nor until the nineteenth century shared in the new magic which emanated from the West would be to answer the central question of medieval history: why the "victory" of Latin Christendom over Greek Christendom and Islam? Time, alas, allows us only to note Western Europe's "victory" and to emphasize that by the time the Muslim had been jolted into the realization that his very survival depended, to large degree, upon his ability to assimilate the new learning and institutions, the West could boast a lead that seemed to be, and may indeed be, too wide for the Muslim world to close.

The Turk stood before Vienna a second time in 1683.

His second failure there was merest indication of things to come. In 1699 the Ottomans were compelled to sign their first treaty concluded with victorious Europeans. Regularity of military disaster was the Muslims' lot in the eighteenth century, reaching a terrible climax in Napoleon's successful invasion of Egypt in 1798. But no mere recital of military defeats and humilating treaties is apt to convey adequately a sense of the psychological dislocation occasioned by the events of the eighteenth and then the nineteenth century, particularly Bonaparte's easy conquest of Egypt. If one leaves aside the infinitely slow Christian reconquest of Spain, the French expedition to Egypt marked the first substantial intrusion of infidel arms into the Muslim heartland since the Crusades. Muslim history had been but for a few episodes a virtually unmitigated success story. Unlike Christianity which had undergone its first three centuries in endemic persecution; had seen the Western Christian Roman Empire disintegrate to Augustine's assurance that such calamity derived after all from our and Adam's curse; had seen the Christian Middle East, North Africa and Spain abandon the Cross for the militant faith of the Arabian Prophet; had endured the failure of the Crusades and the Ottomans plucking the Christian Balkans preparatory to feasting upon the Second Rome itself; had shuddered as the Ottomans twice threatened at Vienna the Habsburg shield which seemed to stand as the only protection against a Muslim invasion of the Latin Christian heartland—unlike Christianity which had known worldly defeat almost as intimately as worldly success, the Muslim world had little in its experience which would have made intelligible, much less tolerable, the catastrophies of the eighteenth and nineteenth centuries. Mundane success had been so generally the fact that it was seen as an altogether natural

46

consequence of Islam's divine election. Among many Muslims the events of the eighteenth and nineteenth centuries imparted fresh significance to words which theretofore had resonated principally among mystics: "This world is the prison of the believers; and the paradise of the unbelievers."[5]

*   *   *

Insofar as the profound confusions which surrounded the activities of Ottoman ruling circles in the nineteenth century allowed direction, that direction led toward two goals: to develop a military establishment that could stave off the Western onslaught and to develop political and legal institutions which could retain the loyalty of Ottoman subjects, not excluding the Balkan Christians who had come to see their redemption in terms of that peculiarly Western institution, the nation-state. The development of a new military establishment was no simple thing. The Turks were to learn that it could not be isolated from, among other things, near-total overhaul of traditional education, until the nineteenth century the virtual monopoly of the religious institution. It is, I think, axiomatic that when modern Western civilization has clashed with another, the result has not been the emergence of a distinct civilization combining the better elements of both. Western civilization has killed or severely crippled the other and insofar as cohabitation occurs it tends to feature some of the worst elements of both. Something like this took place in the Ottoman Empire in the nineteenth century as a Western educational structure came to parallel—and scarcely ever touch—the traditional educational structure. The former functioned as if all learning began with Descartes while the latter assumed

5. Cited in: Bernard Lewis, *The Middle East and the West* (Bloomington, 1964), p. 33.

increasingly a defensive, polemical and hence largely sterile posture—neither the classical, humanistic learning of the Christian West nor the rich classical tradition of Islamic learning. The new education would of course gain the day and succeed slowly in upending the old values and aspirations of Ottoman Muslims. Among non-Muslims this process was merely more rapid and somewhat less jarring. Given the nature of the pressures and the limitations of time, however, the Ottomans failed to develop the ethos and sustain the technology requisite for the emergence of a military machine capable of staying the European hand.

So too with regard to the attempt to evolve new political and legal institutions capable of holding together the multiethnic, multi-linguistic and multi-religious Empire. *Ottomanization*, that ill-fated effort to create a political unity by substituting secular law and allegiance to dynasty for the Islamic definitions, fell before the resentment of Muslims and the refusal of the Balkan Christians to contemplate a political alternative to the nation-state. On the eve of World War I little remained of the Ottoman Empire but the Turkish heartland of Anatolia and the Arab provinces of the Fertile Cresent. Even Egypt, though legally still an Ottoman province, had been, since 1882, occupied by the British.

Not unnaturally the Muslims, Turks as well as Arabs, were the last Ottomans to succumb to the nationalist epidemic. For both peoples the situation was infinitely more complicated than it had been for the Empire's Balkan subjects. In the first place, the men of the Balkans were Christians and, despite Muslim pockets here and there and an Albanian population that was more than half Muslim, the religious and linguistic homogeneity of individual Balkan peoples was considerable. Greeks, Serbs, Rumanians and

48

Bulgars each occupied more or less distinct areas in which distinct languages more or less held sway. And while it may be argued that modern nationalism is hardly less offensive to the Orthodox Christianity to which most Balkan peoples subscribed than it is to Islam, the older faith makes at least the theoretical distinction between what is God's and what is Caesar's—a distinction never admitted in theory and only reluctantly in practice by Islam. Obviously, too, the men of the Balkans were not dismembering an Orthodox Christian Empire, only an Islamic Empire.

The Turks, on the other hand, until the Islamic definitions and their abortive substitute, Ottomanization, had demonstrated their impotence, were not free to develop an unadulterated national consciousness. The same was largely true of the Arab Muslims, although to them Ottomanization held even less appeal than to the Turk. Not burdened with the responsibility of governing, the Arab Muslim could cling a moment longer to the Islamic definitions. Moreover, any ethnic, linguistic or national identity Muslim Turk or Arab possessed was so bound up with Islam as to be virtually indistinguishable from it. Islam had been for each the source of his glory, power and culture. Finally, and this is quite central to the main point I should like to make about the political arrangements of the contemporary and future Middle East, traditional Islamic tolerance had enabled substantial numbers of Greeks and Armenians to remain in Anatolia, in that territory which would have to comprise the Turkish nation-state. Eastern Anatolia displayed the further complication of the Kurd—Muslim, to be sure, but ethnically and linguistically distinct from his Turkish coreligionist. An even older Islamic hegemony than that of the Ottoman had been responsible for the incredibly rich mosaic of ethnicity, language and especially confession which was and remains the Arab Middle East. Even without the predatory territorial ambitions of the European powers, could the sundry indigenous communities of the Middle East be accommodated under the rubric of the nation-state?

Certain Arab Christians thought so and they, rather than their Muslim brethren, exhibited the first nationalist stirrings in the late nineteenth century. For these Christians the formation of a secular nation-state—Lebanese, Syrian or more broadly Arab and patterned after the wonderfully successful Western model—would be the means by which their marginality, their immemorial subordination would be undone; nationalism, in providing a new principle of authority, would create a new community in which they, the Arabic-speaking Christians, could at last function on that level of equality forever denied them by the Muslim definitions. For the Arab Sunni Muslim, on the other hand, nationalism meant not only sharing hegemony with those he had governed for twelve hundred years but doing violence to the spirit and letter of the Divine Law itself. Only by slow degrees, with infinite pain and in the apparent absence of any alternative did the idea of the nation-state find a place in Muslim thought and sensibility. Inevitably, however, the idea would be conceived rather differently by Arab Muslim and Arab Christian. For the latter it implied a truly secular state; for the former something of a secular mutation of Islamic universalism in which Muslim supremacy, though largely undefined, was nonetheless assumed.

As for the Turks, even before World War I destroyed their Empire, the concept of the nation-state had penetrated the mind of an élite conditioned by Western education and example. And while most Muslim Arabs and Turks could clutch yet a while longer the hope that somehow the

Islamic heartland of Anatolia and the Fertile Crescent would continue to reflect the universal Islamic Empire, the Great War seemed to empty that pious aspiration of all substance. The successor states to the Empire of the Ottomans would be nation-states, though such polities had basis neither in Islamic history nor in the contemporary vision of the great majority of Middle Eastern Muslims and, let it be noted, many non-Muslims as well.

*   *   *

The Turkish nation-state was, in the event, forged by the general and spontaneous action of Turks themselves as the victorious European powers prepared the long-deferred internment of "The Sick Man of Europe." Confronted by wartime agreements that would have parcelled Anatolia into several pieces, all but one of them under the overlord-ship of a different European power; confronted as well by a Greek "Zionism" that would have made of western Anatolia the nucleus of a restored Byzantine Empire, the Turks, led by the formidable Mustafa Kemal Ataturk and fighting more as Muslims than as Turks, rid Anatolia of the Greek invaders, foiled the implementation of the Allied agreements and prepared the way for the emergence of the Republic of Turkey.

But if the Turks were to make of Anatolia a Turkish nation-state possessed of that homogeneity characteristic of the more successful European models, there existed three dissonant elements which had to be confronted. These were the Armenians, the Greeks and the Kurds. The Armenians had, in the late nineteenth century, followed the example of the Balkan Christians and agitated for their own homeland in eastern Anatolia. Certain of their leaders, indeed, were not beyond provoking harsh Turkish repression in the hope that the jingoist Western European press would espouse the Armenian nationalist cause as lustily as it had the Greek and Bulgarian after "the massacre of Chios" and "the Bulgarian atrocities." Overlooked by many of the nationalists, however, were two items. The first was that it would prove extremely difficult for any sympathetic Western European power to sail a fleet over the Taurus Range to succor the Armenians; the second was that the Armenians claimed as their homeland an area in which they did not constitute a majority of the population. Armenian leaders, dazzled by the vision of their own nation-state, would, in a sense, co-author their people's ruin. During World War I a number were in open collusion with the Ottoman enemy, Tsarist Russia, and the Ottoman government understandably interpreted this as treason and as a distinct threat to their eastern flank. It was under these circumstances and against the background of several decades of Armenian nationalist agitation that the Turks made their awful resolution to expel the Armenians from their ancient position in Anatolia, driving them southward into the Fertile Crescent. Many, as we know, were lost, though a substantial number made it to these Arab lands to the south, swelling thereby the historic Armenian communities in the Fertile Crescent, enriching and further complicating the mosaic of that area.

For their part, the Greeks of Anatolia were all but eliminated as a result of the abortive invasion of their "conationals" from across the Aegean and in the aftermath of that invasion which saw the Muslims of Greece exchanged for most of the Greek Christians of Anatolia, with all the attendant dislocations and misery for that and the next generation of deportees. I would remark parenthetically that the last scene in this tragedy is now being staged on the island of Cyprus.

52

The Armenians and Greeks of Anatolia, to no small extent because of their own nationalism, were now virtually eliminated. The Turks were left with the Kurds who sit there still in the fastness of eastern Anatolia. Staunch Sunni Muslims, though retaining their distinctive Indo-European tongue, the Kurds constituted no great problem prior to the Great War, for the orthodox Islam common to Turk as well as Kurd cloaked (as universalist religions were perhaps invented to do) the ethnic and linguistic differences. Only as the decades before and following World War I saw the nationalist virus begin to infect the Kurds and intensify among the Turks did hostility become overt. Today the Kurdish problem in the Middle East must rank only behind the Palestine problem in complexity and danger. For the Kurds are not a peculiarly Turkish difficulty. They number several millions, are dispersed in Iraq, Iran and Syria as well as Turkey and the creation of *their* national homeland would necessitate dismemberment of at least three of these states: dismemberments of dismemberment. The point should be obvious but nonetheless let it be made explicit. To satisfy every craving on the part of different Middle Eastern peoples for the nation-state would result—to marked degree has already resulted—in demographic, geographic, political and economic absurdities. On this note let us turn to the contemporary Arab world of the Fertile Crescent—the Arab heartland, as it were.

* * *

I have alluded more than once to the mosaic of peoples making up this "Arab" heartland. Let me now be a bit more specific. Leaving to one side for the moment the Jewish population of Israel, a population which was simply not there until the immigration following World War I, the

53

population of the Fertile Crescent is overwhelmingly Arabic-speaking and perhaps eighty percent Muslim. But Islam here is not a unity. The majority of these Muslims is, to be sure, Sunni or orthodox but there exists as well a sizable minority of heterodox Muslims (themselves fragmented into several groups) and mutual antagonisms have hardly been quieted by decreeing from above that all are members of this or that Arab state or the one Arab state that the future will surely yield. In Iraq, for example, the heterodox are about as numerous as the orthodox though the latter tend to be dominant politically and economically. In Syria today a particular sect of heterodox Muslims—though a relatively small minority in the population at large—enjoys effective control of government and army, to the sustained applause of neither the orthodox Muslim majority nor other heterodox Muslim sects nor the various Christian communities. In Lebanon the heterodox, divided into two main groups, comprise but two of the many pieces making up the inconceivable Lebanese mosaic. And let us remind ourselves that within the orthodox Islam of the Fertile Crescent we have the ethnic and linguistic division and the different national aspirations separating the Kurd from his Arabic-speaking cosectary. The Kurd's territorial ambitions are there for all to contemplate, and where within the concept of the nation-state lies the logic which is to deny him and others their ambitions? Only the variable logic of power. Perhaps what is needed is the logic of communal government inherent in the old Ottoman *millet* system.

As for the Christian population of the Fertile Crescent, mere mention of the distinct Christian confessions to be found there may convey some idea of the difficulty of welding them into a unity with one another, much less with orthodox and heterodox Muslims. There exist Greek Orthodox and Greek Catholics, so-called Syrian Orthodox and Syrian Catholics, Nestorians and Chaldaean Catholics, Armenian Orthodox and Armenian Catholics, a smattering of Latin Catholics and various small Protestant groups of recent vintage. Special mention must of course be made of the Maronites, a largely Lebanese community in communion with Rome, who, in making up some twenty percent of the Lebanese population, loom as the largest single community in the country. The Republic of Lebanon exists, indeed, as testimony to Maronite particularism and this to the occasional despair of many Muslims and more than a few Christians cut from other than Maronite cloth.

It is a commonplace that the survival of the many Christian communities of the Fertile Crescent was due, in the main, to that Islamic tolerance institutionalized, in Ottoman times, through the *millet* system. But now there is no *millet* system granting to each confession its distinct place, its communal autonomy—except, in a much modified manner, within the narrow confines of Lebanon. And to this or that Christian or Muslim community, seemingly clear threats lurk in Lebanese or Syrian, let alone Jewish, nationalism. Pan-Arab nationalism, meanwhile, seems strangely like a cover for the hegemony of the Arab orthodox Muslims, but a hegemony lacking the special arrangements which universalist Islam, before and during its Ottoman expression, had accorded Christians, Jews and even heterodox Muslims. Against this background is it merely fortuitous that the idea of the Arab nation-state has still to be translated into a political unity embracing Lebanon, Syria, Iraq and Jordan, not to mention Palestine and Egypt? Perhaps the very idea of the nation-state, whether pan-Arab or more narrowly defined, needs reconsideration in light of a communal heterogeneity that will not soon disappear.

The casualties associated with Arab nationalism in the Fertile Crescent, while less numerous than those born of Greek, Armenian and Turkish nationalism, nevertheless bear some mention. The ongoing struggle between Kurdish and Arab nationalism, centered for the moment in Iraq, is currently critical and as far from genuine solution as ever. The elimination of most of the Arabic-speaking Jewish communities, through emigration to Israel following the creation of the state in 1948, must count as largely Zionist-inspired but, particularly in Iraq, Arab-encouraged. More of course will be said of the clash between Jewish and Arab nationalism but first let us pause to remember the calamity which befell the Nestorian Christian or "Assyrian" community in Iraq in the early 1930's.

The martial remnant of this ancient community, which in the prime of medieval Islam had still the vigor and Christian vision to send its missionaries as far as China and India (an achievement in itself no mean index to the extent of Islamic tolerance), could be found in Iraq after World War I, stirred by the nationalist idea and serving as auxiliary units in the army of the British Mandate authority. Like a number of minorities in the wake of the Ottoman collapse, these Nestorians understandably feared that they would retain a *de facto* second-class citizenship in the new nation-states being created by the "Balkanization" of the Middle East but without that precious boon of the *millet* system: communal autonomy. Their cleaving to the British while claiming the right to their own homeland (in an area in which they were greatly outnumbered by Muslims) is thus to be explained in terms of a profound apprehension spawned by the Ottoman ruin. This was the stuff of tragedy and surely deserves our sympathetic understanding. But must we not remark with equal sympathy the reaction of the Muslims of Iraq, Arab or Kurd, who came to regard the Nestorians as, variously, lackeys of the mandatory power, traitors to the Iraqi or Arab nation, Christians who, in shaping their own homeland, would lightly dismiss the Muslim Arabs and Kurds immemorially contained therein? The British, however inadvertently, abandoned their erstwhile levies to their fate—as they later abandoned India and Palestine to ill-fated partitions. The Nestorians were the object of a massacre, albeit provoked, at the hands of the new Iraqi army in 1933.

And what of the consequences of the Jewish nationalism which created the Zionist state in Palestine in 1948? For, whatever the origins of the Jewish settlers or their ill-conceived and ill-disguised contempt for the Arabs and the traditional Middle East, the Jews of Israel are very much a part of the Middle Eastern mosaic, and until the confrontation between Arab, or perhaps more precisely *Palestinian* Arab, and Jewish nationalism ends, no Middle Easterner can anticipate any degree of tranquility and order.

Bernard Lewis, the English Jewish scholar of Islam, has written:

Jews are an inventive people. They have been credited, by their more ardent admirers and detractors, with inventing both capitalism and communism, both Christianity and Islam; they did not, however, invent political Zionism.[6]

Political Zionism was born of Central and Eastern European nationalism and the disinclination of Christian nationalists, as well as many Jews amidst them, to accept the proposition that Jews could be truly Germans, Hungarians, Russians or Poles. One may indeed view the fervor and leadership bestowed by Jews upon the early socialist movements

6. Ibid., p. 91.

in Eastern Europe as an attempt to create that elusive universal which would resolve the question of Jewish identity as Central and Eastern European nationalisms had failed to do. That Marxist universalism will succeed in Eastern Europe or the Middle East is at best dubious. For the Marxist demand is for the soul, and it is precisely the soul—the essential identity—of Jew, Kurd and multifarious Arab that will, for the foreseeable future, refuse to yield. Of this essential identity the *millet* system, we should remind ourselves, at least took cognizance. But this is to digress.

Political Zionism, then, originated as a peculiarly European phenomenon, not at all indigenous to the historic Jewish communities of the Arab or Muslim world. And whatever the historic and religious associations of the Jews with Palestine, it is a salient fact that when the modern Zionist turned his gaze toward Palestine, that land had been non-Jewish for almost two thousand years and Arab or arabized for over twelve hundred years. The Jews of Palestine, at the close of World War I, comprised a mere seven percent of the population of the Holy Land, and most of that seven percent harbored few Zionist aspirations. This is not the time to trace the course of the Jewish emigration from Europe to Palestine, largely as a result of the Fascist barbarism, nor the furious but ineffectual opposition of the indigenous Arabs, nor the inner contradictions which, from the outset, tore the policy of the mandatory power, Great Britain, nor the apparent victory of Jewish nationalism in Palestine and the consequent expulsion and flight of much of the Arab population of the Holy Land. But two points deserve emphasis: the first is that although the Arabs of Palestine were called upon to pay the price for the plight of European Jewry—Christian anti-semitism, if such it was, and the post-Christian gas chamber had nothing to do with the Arab or Muslim worlds—the Jews *are* in Palestine and this must be a working assumption in constructing the future institutional arrangements of the entire Middle East; the second is that the Palestinian Arabs have a claim against the Jewish state that must and will somehow be honored. There is no acceptable military solution to the conflict between Palestinian Arab and Jewish nationalists, and to the extent that a military solution exists at all it is not apt to favor the latter.[7] In sum, neither Zionist nor Palestinian nor yet any other nationalist in the Fertile Crescent has been, or will be, able to achieve his ends without intolerable injury to others whose claims lack only the logic of power. But power, it need hardly be remarked, does not ordinarily remain the monopoly of any single group.

Is it too far-fetched to suggest that the same Islamic tolerance largely responsible for the communal survival of most of those comprising the Middle Eastern mosaic also devised certain institutional arrangements which, adapted and modified today, might provide an alternative to the essentially retrogressive pattern of the nation-state? Is it possible that a "neo-*millet* system," implemented by a unitary Fertile Crescent state, might provide not only a secure degree of communal autonomy to each element of the mosaic but even that first-class citizenship which the Islamic definitions could grant only to Muslims? I do not need to be reminded of the difficulties we face in accepting once more an "internationalism" until we have been spent in a parochial and poisonous struggle for national self-assertion. Nor do I need a reminder that the *millet* system presupposed the cement of Islamic ideology and a Muslim center of power and decision-making. And it is only in this immediate context

7. The events of and subsequent to October 1973 have served only to confirm this assessment.

that I mean to beg the question of how the men of the Middle East might go about ushering in the brave new world, the limitations of time obviously standing between me and the appropriate speculation. I mean only to suggest that it may be time to speak of the Fertile Crescent in terms other than the inevitability of contending nationalisms. I mean to suggest too that should the Fertile Crescent fail to devise some viable adaptation of the old *millet* arrangements, that area and the super-powers engaged therein may look forward to a deepening of the chaos which has been characteristic since the fracture of the Ottoman peace. Such a future is not to be contemplated with equanimity.

I would close with a gentle admonition to hear the words of Elie Kedourie, that embittered Mesopotamian—let us call him, despite his or others' disclaimers, that Arab Jew— who has described so poignantly his own community's disintegration in the crossfire between Jewish and Arab nationalism:

> The improvement of conditions in the east needed knowledge, good-will and patience; the statesmen and diplomats who undertook the task were, for the most part, ignorant, indifferent and in a hurry; or if not indifferent then seized with unwholesome passions for Ottoman or Armenian, Arab or Zionist. Hence the atrocities incident to national self-determination, the destruction of those small, frail communities with very limited political experience, who were unable to deal with such new and terrifying manifestations, and the origin of those perverted commonwealths of the east to which no good man can give his loyalty. The measure of the failure is that today the west should be exhorted to build in the east nations where 'Moslems, Christians and Jews can and will live in harmony.' The Ottoman state was organized in such a way as to fulfil precisely this requirement.

> The Ottoman system was far from perfect. It was narrow and

hidebound. It knew nothing of the richness, the flexibility and the opportunities existing in the western tradition. But its conventions were well established and its modalities well understood. In due course, the habits perhaps would be capable of being fostered,

that made old wrong
Melt down as it were wax in the sun's rays.[8]

Robert M. Haddad

8. Kedourie, pp. 315–316.

THE CLASH OF EMPIRES:
PERU'S ENDURING PARADOX

THE CLASH OF EMPIRES:
PERU'S ENDURING PARADOX

O N the morning of October 3, 1968, the Peruvian nation awoke to the announcement that it had a new military government. During the night, the Lima Armoured Division tanks had surrounded the government palace, aroused the guards and informed the Constitutional President of Peru, Fernando Belaúnde Terry, that his administration was over. The military officers took Belaúnde to the Lima airport and spirited him away to Argentina, alive and well. In the best etiquette of South American coups not a shot was fired, no struggle took place.

Since that day in October five years ago Peruvians have lived under what has come to be called the Revolutionary Government of the Armed Forces. In a series of sweeping actions this government set about reorganizing the structures and institutions of Peruvian society, announcing reforms in industry, mining, banking and agriculture. The first and perhaps the most important was the agrarian reform.

Peru's President, Juan Velasco Alvarado, indicated the primacy of this reform in his promulgation speech:

Faithful to our mission to the country and to history, and to the explicit goals of the Revolution, the government of the armed forces today is adopting an agrarian reform law that will mark the beginning of the true liberation of the Peruvian peasant. . . .

Answering the clamor for justice and the rights of the neediest, the agrarian reform law supports the great mass of peasants who form the Indian communities. . . . We believe that we will carry out a duty to make restitution to all those forgotten peasants of Peru who for centuries have suffered all kinds of exploitation and injustice.[1]

Velasco's remarks express a continuing theme in Peruvian politics. They echo previous words expressing the hopes and desires of earlier leaders: the hope that they could untangle the enduring paradox in national Peruvian life which arises from the clash between the Spanish and Inca Empires. To understand Peruvian history and its present politics one must appreciate the lasting antagonisms set in motion when the Inca and Spanish Empires clashed in 1531.

The problems which grew out of this initial conflict of Empires are still the critical ones posed to the Revolutionary Government of the Armed Forces. Paradoxically, that government's ability to resolve this historical conflict will be the measure of its revolutionary claims. Simply put, the degree to which the present government of Peru can be considered revolutionary is the degree to which it is able to come to terms with its past.

In Peru, to come to terms with the past means to come to terms with the rural Indian sector of society. In its most general form the question is: what is to be done with the rural sierra? Policy toward the sierra has been a source of

1. Juan Velasco Alvarado, June 24, 1969, from his speech announcing the agrarian reform, as reported in *Oiga* (Lima) June 27, 1969, translated and reprinted in Paul Sigmund, ed., *The Ideologies of the Developing Nations*, 2d ed. rev. (New York: Praeger, 1972), pp. 400–401.

political cleavage in Peru and remains unresolved.[2] It is complicated by the racial cleavage between rural Indian Peru and coastal mestizo society. The lack of resolution is related to the aftermath of Empire, to the controversies growing out of interpretations of the clash of Empires in Peru in the sixteenth century. The ramifications of these diverse interpretations of the conquest can be traced throughout the Colonial and Republican periods and into the twentieth century. Political leaders from the remarkable Viceroy Toledo[3] through Belaúnde Terry and most recently Juan Velasco Alvarado have struggled, with varying degrees of dedication and skill to come to grips with the issues inherent in the clash of these two Empires.

2. In 1965 Patch wrote:
"Thus Peru has not only the problems common to all Latin American countries: poverty, landlessness, illiteracy and growing unemployed populations in the largest cities; it also has the problem that nearly a half of its people do not participate in the nation. Their economy is subsistence, and their political activity is limited to occasional revolts against landowners. Their society and their culture are not those of the Spanish speakers who consider themselves 'Peruvian.' Some Peruvians even consider the *Indios* an inferior aboriginal race.

"This is the problem facing Fernando Belaúnde and his government—how to construct a nation which has meaning for all, not half, of the persons who are born and live within its territorial boundaries." (Richard W. Patch, "A Note on Bolivia and Peru," *American University Field Staff Reports*, West Coast of South America series, 2 [1965], p. 21.)

For a more recent treatment of the same problem as it is faced by the military government see Susan C. Bourque and David Scott Palmer, "Transforming the Rural Sector: Government Policy and Peasant Response," a paper delivered at the Seminar on Continuity and Change in Contemporary Peru, Center for Inter-American Relations, New York City, June 1, 1973.

3. For a discussion of Toledo's policies see Lewis Hanke, *The Spanish Struggle for Justice in the Conquest of America* (Philadelphia: Univ. of Pennsylvania, 1949), chap. XII, pp. 162–172.

The Spaniards and Incas were not simply warring groups competing for an attractive piece of property. More important in the long run, the two Empires represented distinct ways of organizing economic and political life, they professed different religions, spoke different languages and organized their societies around different goals. When they confronted one another it was a genuine cultural clash, a clash with deep economic and political undergirdings. It is not surprising that the conflicts have endured and are writ large in the present controversy over the direction of Peruvian society.

The issues for modern Peruvians turn on the proper interpretation of the characteristics of the Spanish and Inca Empires: which Empire offered the best option, which was the most efficiently organized, the best administered, which pursued the loftiest goals and which offered a better way of life to the individuals who fell within its sway.

The conflict over the quality of each Empire is the source of the modern nation's problem. There are no common heroes, and no common villains. Indeed, one person's hero becomes another's villain. Nor is there agreement about the events of the past, what they signal or how one feels about them.[4] For some Peruvians the fall of the Inca Empire is tragedy. It is that moment in the past which they can identify as the source of modern Peruvian problems. Indeed they argue that solutions to the critical problems facing the nation today can be found in a re-emphasis of Inca values and practices.[5]

4. Frederick B. Pike, *The Modern History of Peru* (London: Weidenfeld and Nicolson, 1967), p. 6.
5. One finds elements of this in early *Agrista* ideology, and to some degree in the statements of Belaúnde and the present government. For a full discussion see Pike, *The Modern History of Peru*, par-

For other Peruvians the Spanish conquest marks the moment when civilization arrives. They see the Spanish influence as Peru's tie to the modern world, the open window through which the nation escaped from the hold of pagan superstition to rational intercourse with an advanced Christian culture.[6]

The conflict of Empires reflects not only the loss of a national glue (a common sense of history and core of beliefs about the nation's sources of pride), it also gives rise to substantive policy questions. One cannot decide on the best policy for the rural areas without resolving the question of the relative contributions of the Inca and Spanish Empires in that sector. The two civilizations dealt with the rural sector in distinct fashions for it was attributed widely different priority by each group.

A complicating factor in the case of Peru is the level at which these questions are debated and the intensity of the dispute. Academics who delight in this type of controversy have unfortunately carried their debates into the realm of public policy. History becomes the arena for an ongoing polemic, but polemic with rather serious consequences for

---

ticularly chap. 1 and pp. 234–235, 307. Pike writes of Valcárcel, an *indigenista* and gifted writer of the 1920's: . . . "Valcárcel saw the future not in terms of a synthesis, but in the imposition by the Indian of his civilization, pure and uncontaminated, on all Peru and all Latin America, or, as he preferred to call it, Indo-America. 'European culture,' he wrote, 'has never truly affected the Indian. Peru is Indian and will be Indian. . . . The only true Peru is Indian Peru' " (p. 234).

6. Pike, *The Modern History of Peru*, pp. 14–15. His quotation from Herrera is instructive: "The work which the Spanish accomplished . . . was the greatest work which the Almighty has accomplished through the hands of men. . . . to infuse this world with Christianity, to introduce the fire of life into millions of moribund souls, to broaden by millions of leagues the sphere of human intelligence, was an accomplishment of unparalleled splendour."

the nation. One North American historian commented on Peruvian history in this fashion:

As has been true of the approach to the Inca past, colonial history will serve largely to prevent the emergence of widely shared values and sentiments, thus holding Peruvians back in their search for a nation. Events of the past will not be studied in the light of how they have contributed to or retarded the emergence of the securely-established main features of present-day life. Instead, they will be seized upon as justification for passionate crusades seeking to influence the still-to-be resolved character of modern existence.[7]

The past becomes the vehicle to justify the programs and policies of today. That is not inherently untenable. However, the fundamental controversy complicates the policy dimension: there is no consensus over how to interpret the past. Historians and anthropologists disagree about the nature of both the Spanish and Inca Empires.

The Inca Empire is subject to the most widely divergent interpretations. It has been described as: a socialistic heaven, a despotic dictatorship, a marvel of mass egalitarian organization and a strictly stratified hierarchical autocracy. One social scientist with a flair for inclusion submitted this description:

Socialism, linked with democracy in Marxian theory, was consistent in Peru with monarchy and aristocracy. The Inca system exerted a leveling influence, creating a uniform standard of living throughout the empire. If it thus realized the ideal equality, it was equality only within a given social class.[8]

It is evident that individuals choosing to evoke images of the past have a wide variety of myths to choose from and

7. Ibid., pp. 19–20.
8. Murdock, quoted in: Sally Falk Moore, *Power and Property in Inca Peru* (New York: Columbia Univ. Press, 1958), p. 6.

can select those which best serve their purpose. Nevertheless, there are a few generally accepted aspects of the Inca past which are useful in assessing the problems of the present.

The Inca Empire was, first of all, a relatively new Empire. It had consolidated its power only ninety years previous to the arrival of the Spanish. It was also a huge Empire. At its zenith it reached from the northern border of Ecuador, south through Peru to Chile, and east to Bolivia. Its center, geographically and politically, was Cuzco in the southern sierra regions of Peru. Somewhere between three and six million subjects lived within its confines.

The Incas expanded from their base in southern Peru, extending their control in the usual fashion of Empires, through conquest. It is argued with some persuasion that the Incas brought peace to the Andes. The imposition of their control, so the argument goes, brought an end to the intervillage rivalry, looting and burning which existed in some regions. On the other hand, the Incas conquered several highly advanced societies, most notably those of the Peruvian coast, the Chimu. Rather than an uncivilized tribe, the Chimu had established a large and well-ordered kingdom, with a prosperous population of over 100,000 living in an urbanized setting.[9]

The evidence indicates that the Incas had a very efficient system of administration over these vast territories. They kept close account of agricultural production and population. They demanded tribute from their subjects, and a part

9. For a full account of the groups conquered by the Inca, see John Howland Rowe, "Inca Culture at the Time of the Spanish Conquest," in *Handbook of South American Indians*, Vol. 2, *The Andean Civilizations*, Julian Steward, ed., Smithsonian Institution, Bureau of American Ethnology, *Bulletin* 143 (Washington, D.C.: U.S. Government Printing Office, 1946), pp. 201–207.

of the land was tilled for the Sun, or the Inca, the Sun's governmental representative. It appears that the Incas were not adamant about the acceptance of their religious practices by the peoples they conquered. They were far more concerned that the conquered demonstrate political loyalty. They were quite willing to punish whole communities if they resisted Inca rule.[10]

The Empire was unified by a series of roads which ran its length and breadth. The roads were furnished with a system of runners, *chasquis*, who carried messages, recorded on *quipus*, throughout the kingdom. There is good evidence that the Incas had established a system to assure the distribution of food throughout the Empire. Thus a region hit by bad weather or poor crops would not experience famine, but could be relieved through the community stores of grain.[11]

The Inca leadership imposed a strict code of conduct on their subjects, a code that did not apply to the leadership itself. One scholar notes:

How significant that penalties for all crimes were lighter for the nobility, that what was criminal for the commoner was often not so for the noble, that nobles could expect to be judged by their peers, and that the Inca enjoyed the greatest privilege of all, being virtually incapable of crime, since from incest to homicide . . . the Inca emperor was not bound by the rules which bound others.[12]

This Empire was a mix of several elements. Clearly it was not egalitarian and the authority of the Inca rulers was extensive. On the other hand it appears to have been organized around a recognition of the needs of its subjects and a concern for the public good. There were considerable de-

10. Rowe, "Inca Culture," pp. 269–270.
11. Ibid., p. 231, 255, 265–267.
12. Moore, *Power and Property in Inca Peru*, p. 134.

mands made of the subjects: taxes were levied, a proportion of production was reserved for the Inca[13] and the roads, public works, and fortresses throughout the nation were built by drafted labor.[14]

One cannot assess the Inca situation (even in the brief sketch offered here) without some appreciation of the Spanish alternative. The nature of Spanish rule is central to our understanding of the conflict between the two Empires. The initial question might be: Did the Spanish alter anything other than the leadership? It has been argued that the Spanish conquest represented nothing more than the substitution of one élite group for another: the Inca clan is exchanged for the emissaries of the Spanish Crown.[15] After all, so the argument runs, the Incas came to power through conquest no less brutal than that of the Spanish. One author draws this parallel between the two Empires:

[The Incas conceived] of themselves as the essential civilizers of the Andean area.

This, even though there were high civilizations and developed governments before them. From the evidence of the chroniclers, they considered themselves great altruistic statesmen and peace bringers. . . . How fitting that the Inca should in their turn have been conquered by a handful of the most fortune-hunting of Spaniards in the name of true religion, true morality, and true civilization.[16]

13. Ibid., pp. 48–72. Rowe, "Inca Culture," p. 266.

14. Rowe, "Inca Culture," p. 267.

15. Most sources agree that the maintenance of the Inca hierarchy was extremely useful in facilitating Spanish domination. Moreover, Lockhart argues that Spanish society was simply transferred overseas. In the Peruvian case: " . . . an essentially intact, complete Spanish society was transferred to Peru in the conquest and civil war period" (James Lockhart, *Spanish Peru 1532–1560* [Madison: Univ. of Wisconsin Press, 1968], p. 221).

16. Moore, op. cit., pp. 134–135.

The parallel is instructive. It focuses our attention on the Spaniards' motives. As in the case of the Incas' conviction that they were altruistic civilizers, segments of the Spanish community were concerned with the well-being of the groups they subjugated. Many Spaniards felt their desire to christianize the pagan Indians was an end which justified war. In the years preceding the conquest of Peru and throughout the sixteenth century there was a heated debate in Spain over the justice of the conquest. Members of the clergy, in particular, were concerned about adequate protection of the conquered populations. Were the Indians treated fairly? Had the proper laws been adopted?[17] A sector of the clergy frequently denounced the actions of the conquistadors. The nature of the Indian civilizations was debated in the highest circles of government. The Spanish treated this as a serious question and in the early years of the conquest tried to resolve it through legislative efforts.[18]

Despite the efforts of part of the Spanish community the Indians did not fare well under the conquest. Here is a nineteenth-century Peruvian president's assessment:

The conquest opened to the Indian a new era of slavery, one that was more severe than the slavery he had previously endured. While despots, the Inca rulers had been solicitous for the welfare of their subjects; but the newcomers cared little for their wards. In spite of all legal attempts to protect them, the Indians were slaves.[19]

17. For a full discussion see Lewis Hanke, *The Spanish Struggle for Justice*, passim.

18. The Requirement, the Laws of Burgos, and the New Laws were all serious attempts on the part of the Council of the Indies to ensure just Spanish behavior toward the Indians. For a full discussion of these legislative efforts see Hanke, *The Spanish Struggle for Justice*, chaps. I–III and VII.

19. "Francisco Garcia Calderón, an eminent nineteenth-century lawyer-statesman and for a short time President of Peru (1881)," as quoted in Pike, *The Modern History of Peru*, pp. 18–19.

Paradoxically the deteriorating condition of the Indians often resulted from the misuse and manipulation of laws which were intended to protect them. This misuse and manipulation was exacerbated by the economic and political changes which accompanied the conquest. The consequences of this economic and political shift are manifold and still plague society.

The Spanish conquest introduced Peru into world trade as part of a mercantilist system. This occasioned a violent re-orientation of an economy which up until that time had been based on agriculture. With the advent of the Spanish, the emphasis turned to mining. This necessitated taking individuals away from agricultural pursuits and putting them into the mines. Agriculture itself underwent change as the Spanish tried to produce foods they had known in Europe. While this had positive aspects in the variety which was introduced, the lasting consequences were negative: agricultural production dropped. Peru began to import food, and famine hit areas of the country as the Inca system of food storage and distribution became defunct.[20]

Concomitantly there were massive demographic changes in the Andes. Estimates vary, but it seems reasonable to conclude that the indigenous population of the Andes was halved in the thirty years after the conquest. Epidemics do not account for the rapid population decline in Peru (though elsewhere in the Americas this was the case). Work in the mines brought with it a heavy death toll. In addition the forced labor recruited for the mines took the Indians away from their agricultural pursuits. This switch dramatically altered the agricultural structure and threw off the precari-

20. George Kubler, "The Quechua in the Colonial World," *Handbook of South American Indians*, op. cit., pp. 342–347.

ous balance which the Incas had constructed to feed the Empire.[21]

As the Peruvian economy geared for participation in world trade and began exporting to the world market, the heart of Peru—the seat of government—moved from the interior in the high sierra regions of Cuzco to coastal Lima. With the change in the capital there was a commensurate re-ordering of government priorities. After the Spanish conquest the coast and Lima became Peru. The hinterland, or sierra, was essential only insofar as it supplied Lima with the necessities of life: precious metals for trade, Indian labor for the mines and domestic service, and cheap food through the maintenance of a thoroughly controlled work force in a feudal agricultural structure.[22]

This work force was created and maintained by three Spanish institutions, two of which were intended to provide some protection and instruction for the Indian population. In actuality they facilitated exploitation.

The *encomienda* was one such institution. It was the Crown's grant of land along with the labor of the Indians found on that land to a Spaniard in payment for meritori-

21. Ibid., pp. 334–339.
22. Pike records some of the extreme expressions of the sierra coastal split. Here are some of the anti-coastal attitudes:
The poet Rodriguez: "I do not even want to hear mentioned the name of Lima, whose existence in its present form I execrate. . . . It is the focal point of the degeneration of our nationality" (*The Modern History of Peru*, p. 235).
"When Lima's daily *El Comercio* criticized the excessively regionalistic and combative spirit of the new [Andean] periodical and went on to say that Peru would be better off without its sierra region, *La Sierra* [the Andean periodical] retorted: 'When it comes to deciding if Peru would be more fortunate without the sierra or without the coast, it can be demonstrated that it would be much more fortunate without the coast'" (*The Modern History of Peru*, p. 235).

ous service. The *encomendero* was expected to educate, christianize and generally protect the Indians, who then provided him with tribute and labor. Lockhart writes:

The encomienda, as is well known, was the basic instrument of Spanish exploitation of Indian labor and produce in the conquest period.[23]

When *encomiendas* bordered on freeholding Indian communities there was a persistent pattern of encroachment by the *encomenderos* on Indian lands. This was facilitated by their access to the judicial system as well as their control of the police power of Spanish administration.[24] Lockhart identifies this trend:

Encomenderos, leaping over technicalities, made their encomiendas the basis of great estates even if they did not legally own the land.[25]

A second institution was the *reducción*. Essentially this was the creation of a new town for the ostensible purpose of bringing together groups of Indians from the outlying areas to instruct them in Spanish and Catholicism. In practice the *reducción* was a mechanism which allowed the Spanish to keep the Indians in close check and away from their land for an impractical period of time. Many returned

23. Lockhart, *Spanish Peru*, p. 11.
24. For a full discussion of the structure and distribution of power in rural Peru see any of the following: Fernando Fuenzalida, "La estructura de la Comunidad Indigenas tradicionales," in R. Keith, *El Campesino en el Peru*, Peru Problema no. 3, IEP (Lima, 1970), pp. 61–104; Julio Cotler, "Actuales Pautas de cambio en la sociedad rural del Peru," in Jose Matos Mar, *Dominación y cambios en el Peru rural*, IEP (Lima, 1969), pp. 60–79; Magali Larson and Arlene Bergman, *Social Stratification in Peru*, Politics of Modernization Series no. 5 (Institute of International Studies, University of California, Berkeley, 1969).
25. Lockhart, *Spanish Peru*, p. 11n.

home to find that their property had been appropriated by a Spaniard.

A third institution, the *mita*, had the same effect as the *reducción*. It removed large sections of the Indian population from their property for up to a year. The *mita* was draft Indian labor provided to work the mines. It was a carry-over from Inca civilization but on a massive scale unknown during pre-colonial days. To meet the demands for labor, entire sections of an Indian community, along with children, animals and household goods would journey several hundred miles, taking up to two months to arrive at the work site. They were expected to work four months and then spend another two months to go home again. If they lived through it, the better part of a year was spent away from their home and property. Many Indians, fearing that they had already lost their land, or alternatively that they might again be subject to the *mita* when it returned to their community, opted not to return home.[26]

All three institutions effectively separated the Indians from the land, or, if maintaining the Indian on it, established Spanish dominance over it. Whatever initial superiority the Spaniards had in firepower was vastly expanded by their steady encroachment on the land. In effect they came to dominate the basis of the Indians' livelihood. They removed the Indian from the most productive land forcing indigenous communities to retreat to the worst and least profitable, or they established direct control over the Indians' labor through the *encomienda* and later *hacienda*. The ability of the Spaniards to impose their will, to take control of the economic resources of the society and determine their exploitation, was an outgrowth of their control of the police and judicial powers of the state. Indians soon learned

26. Kubler, "Colonial Quechua," p. 373.

that in any contest involving the state apparatus they were not the equals of the Spaniards.

In sum, the clash of Empires set in motion two forces which have had enduring impact on modern Peruvian society. First, there was a reorientation of the economy. The wealth base of the Indians was appropriated by the Spaniards. Moreover, through institutions such as the *mita* and *encomienda* a few were allowed to exploit the labor of many. This was true under the Incas as well. But it was not, to the best of our knowledge, carried on in a fashion which allowed for the impoverishment of large sectors of the society. The evidence indicates the contrary: the Inca Empire was organized to avoid this eventuality. Under the Spanish new economic priorities and demands took precedence over this concern. After the conquest, Peru became involved in world trade and her economy geared to those demands.

Concomitantly the focus of political, economic and cultural life moved from the Andes to the coast. The direction and development of the economy were dictated by the needs of the coast, rather than the needs of the whole society. The outcome of this trend was a bifurcation in that society, a rent in the body politic wherein those who were non-Indian enjoyed power and authority over those who were not. The rural Indian population was treated as chattel and systematically deprived of the means through which they could reverse their condition of poverty and exploitation.

Politically the Indian was disenfranchised. The literacy requirement in Spanish excluded the Indian from electoral participation. Moreover, the transfer of political authority to a coastally focused élite (who viewed the Indian majority as a threat to their dominance) curtailed major development efforts in the rural sierra areas. Ignoring this sector, except when shoring up the privileges of non-Indians who wanted to exercise power in the sierra, systematically reduced the Indians to poverty. Their only vehicle for protesting injustice was periodic outbursts of violence which usually exposed them to further repression.

The underdevelopment of the rural sector is the most concrete example of a much deeper societal problem: how are Peruvians to forge a national identity which will include all sectors—both Indian and non-Indian? What economic and social programs can they adopt which will allow for a better distribution of their goods and fuller participation from all citizens? Politicians have focused on the resolution of the rural issues as the key to unraveling the less tangible cultural dimensions of the puzzle. It is the most obvious, palpable outgrowth of a far deeper national paradox.

However, the political system has been unable to resolve even the rural issue. No political party or leader has found a way to knit together the various strands of Peruvian society and redesign it into a pattern which provides for the well-being of the entire population.

This failure is not due to lack of effort. Throughout the twentieth century there have been Peruvian leaders who have sought to resolve questions about the direction of the economy, the integration of urban and rural regions, and exploitation of one group at the hands of another. We find these issues raised by Gonzalez Prada, José Mariategui, Haya de la Torre and Fernando Belaúnde Terry.

All of these Peruvians recognized that to some extent their difficulties related to the clash which took place between the two Empires in the sixteenth century, and the choices that were made as a result of the Spanish victory. All of them recognized that there might have been a different path for Peru. They searched for another choice.

They argued that a better choice would of necessity be based on some meaningful blending of the legacies of both the Spanish and Inca Empires, but a blending which would redress the imbalance between the Indian and non-Indian sectors.[27] Formulating and implementing policy which will allow for that blend is the task that faces the present military government.

The revolutionary character of this regime will not be determined by the role of the military within its institutions, the amount of gunfire expended, or the fact that it takes power through force. What would make the label of revolutionary appropriate would be this government's success in dealing with its dual tradition. In Peru the paradox of revolutionary action is not to make something new, but rather to deal with what has been. If this government is successful then we will have seen a most remarkable event: making a past conflict into the foundation of a unified nation.[28]

Susan C. Bourque

27. Pike has this to say about Belaúnde Terry's efforts to achieve a synthesis: "[Belaúnde] . . . did not insist, in his zeal for change, either on forcing the coastal way of life on the sierra or in imposing the sierra cultural patterns on the coast. He envisioned a genuinely pluralistic country in which the coast could advance with its westernized capitalist traditions while the sierra progressed through its at least semi-socialistic Inca customs. . . . Belaúnde called upon the native communities to advance themselves through the energetic use of the same methods employed by their distant ancestors" (*The Modern History of Peru*, p. 307). A rather similar case can be made for the other Peruvian leaders. Haya de la Torre and the *Aprista* party are illustrative of the difficulties which a group seeking this type of synthesis is likely to encounter.

28. It is still too early to assess the military government's record. Policy is still in its formative stages. Symbolically the government has made it clear that it is concerned with the rural areas and the improvement of the lot of the Indian population.

FROM EMPIRE TO NATION:
THE AFRICAN EXPERIENCE

FROM EMPIRE TO NATION:
THE AFRICAN EXPERIENCE

IT is my honor and privilege to present this the fourth Alumnae College Lecture in homage to my friend and colleague Professor Max Salvadori, Dwight Morrow Professor of History. Professor Salvadori and I have several experiences in common. We have both secluded ourselves in antiquated offices in Seelye Hall, far from the maddening crowd of Wright Hall. He, steadfastly, has rejected the presence of a telephone in his inner sanctum. Coward that I am, I have been seduced by the tinkle of Mr. Bell's naughty nuisance. Professor Salvadori and I both have degrees from the University of Geneva in Switzerland, and we both have first-hand familiarity with East Africa where he lived and worked from 1934 to 1937 and where I arrived for the first time in 1965.

In the years 1934 to 1937, the European empire system, as manifested in black sub-Saharan Africa, was at its zenith, and was not expected to come down from that lofty height for a very long time. If it were to come tumbling down, Evelyn Waugh wrote mischievously in his novel *Black Mischief*, the consequences would be a comic opera in black face. To the surprise of many, including the overwhelming majority of Africans themselves, the European system of Empires in Africa, which seemed so secure in the period between the two World Wars, by 1965 had ceased to exist. And in its place was not so much a comic opera as elements of a tragic drama.

85

The roots of the drama are to be found not only during the colonial era but also in the era prior to the white man's establishing permanent residence on the continent. In the pre-colonial era, Africans had fought with, conquered and enslaved their neighbors depending upon the codes of behavior inherent in the victorious group. Kingdoms evolved which were hierarchically structured, and a system of centralized government developed. Law and order were maintained by a system of adjudication which was established in a written language or in the memories of men whose responsibility it was to pass on this aspect of oral history to their successors. Kingdoms, however, were not the most prevalent systems of government in pre-colonial black Africa.

There were groups, which anthropologists have called tribes, which, because of similarities in language, heritage and values with other tribes, viewed each other as kinsmen in a loose system, which contained little of the sophisticated mechanisms found in kingdom societies. They were autonomous political units existing side by side over considerable land areas, without the domination of one group by another. Theirs was a decentralized system of government.

Lastly, there were peoples, such as the Bushmen of southern Africa, who belonged neither to kingdoms nor to tribal aggregations but to small groups referred to as bands. In some instances, however, these bands because of mutual convenience or through conquest or capture became slaves or persons of inferior status in larger, more complex African political societies. These bands were culturally homogeneous and were characterized by face-to-face social relationships. There was no internal political differentiation, as bands were composed of families that lacked political identity as separate units. Often the eldest male was the leader of the band. While this position of leadership usually passed from father to son, it frequently fell to the one deemed most capable. By hunting and gathering animals, roots and berries these bands survived. Caste and class were absent and economic distinctions were rare, as there was a strong sense of sharing food, water and goods.

It was these disparate types of societies—kingdoms, tribal conglomerates and bands—that European colonialism brought together under a single administrative system. In other words, European Empires in Africa created plural societies where previously only in kingdoms had pluralism evolved to any significant degree. One of the most basic problems facing independent African states today is this legacy of imposed pluralism. Modern African states face the problem that as to culture, values, history and even language, heterogeneity rather than homogeneity is the salient characteristic of their citizenry. Furthermore, pluralism is a problem because during the era of European Empires in black Africa little or nothing was done to blend—to integrate—these diverse units into a viable union.

The causes of the dismemberment of the European Empires in Africa were many, but certainly the primary catalyst was the second World War. After 1945, colonialism was no longer morally defensible. A new commitment emerged in its place to guarantee the universal rights of men to self-determination and self-government. Experience, some might say expediency, rather than ethics prompted this change in attitude. Colonial powers, faced with the formidable tasks of rehabilitating and reconstructing their own national communities and economies, could no longer afford to retain their colonial possessions. The "cost" of doing so increasingly outweighed the rewards of such an endeavor because of the pressure being exerted in both non-colonial Western and anti-colonial non-Western countries, as well as pressure from within the colonial dependencies themselves.

During the war itself, Japanese occupation of Southeast Asia, riding the crest of Japanese military might, shattered the mystique of Western white supremacy. Moreover, the second World War resulted in the shift of world power centers from Western Europe to the United States and the Soviet Union. These two leviathans, having been strange bedfellows during the war, became fierce protagonists after the war in an ideological struggle which was fought in a global arena. In pursuit of adherents to their ideological tenets, each courted the favor of peoples not yet committed to one or the other—and most of these peoples lived under European imperial domination. The continuation of colonialism, therefore, was not in their best interest, although the United States was less vigorous in its admonition against the system than was the Soviet Union. The Asians and Arabs were the first to revolt successfully against colonial rule, and their revolts stimulated Africans towards a more active anti-colonialism and a more effective nationalism.

Nationalism in black Africa was mainly the desire of a Western-educated élite to have an independent government, in order to control and direct the destiny of their territory. The nationalists' primary aim, therefore, was to drive European rulers out of African countries. The campaign was never called anti-Empire but, rather, anti-colonial. Modern African nationalism, for which colonialism was the catalyst, has its roots in the religious separatist movements which were initiated in South Africa in the latter part of the nineteenth century, and which flourished in West and Central Africa until well after the second World War. It was in religious separatist movements that many

Africans sought and found an outlet for the frustrations which they attributed to colonial domination. Africans, brought up in the pervasive religious atmosphere of their own traditional societies, were ready to follow African prophets who expressed a determination to change Protestant Christianity into a fundamentalist African faith. They broke away from white-dominated Protestant churches to establish black-dominated ones. Their leaders preached the gospel of a black heaven, governed by a black Christ and inhabited by black angels. With fiery rhetoric they persuaded their followers that they were the lost children of God, oppressed by white taskmasters.

European missionaries and colonialists panicked and pressed the colonial governments to act. And act they did, especially as some of these separatist church leaders incited their followers to employ violent means in order to redress social injustices. For instance, there was the case of John Chilembwe, a Nÿasa African from what is today called Malawi. At the end of the nineteenth century Chilembwe attended a black college in the southern United States. He returned to Africa impassioned with the belief in African freedom and black renaissance. He founded the Providence Industrial Mission in Malawi, where his preaching attracted a great following. After the outbreak of the first World War, Chilembwe denounced British plans to draft Africans from Malawi to fight German troops in the neighboring German colony of Tanganyika. He lamented: "We have been invited to shed our innocent blood in this World War. In time of peace everything for Europeans only. And instead of honor we suffer humiliation with names contemptible. But in time of war it is found that we are needed to share hardships and shed our blood—in equality."

Chilembwe's lament went unheeded, and in 1915 he led

89

an armed revolt against the British. It failed and he was killed. But the spirit of African resistance did not die with him, although the uprising he led did, in a sense, mark the end of an era. For by 1920, European control was well established in Africa, and increasingly many Africans diverted their energies towards working within the colonial system. They accepted European domination as a situation from which they could acquire certain skills in order to survive and perhaps advance their societies. Europeans interpreted this change in behavior as indicative of their superiority, and testimony to the righteousness of their cause to—as they put it—civilize the Africans. As a consequence, officials of colonial administrations proceeded to strengthen their contact with Africans by involving them in the administrative process. Colonial officials sought Africans to assist in local government, although most often it was more like local control than local government. Many traditional leaders accepted judicial, financial and police responsibilities, which were performed with varying degrees of autonomy. This involvement in the colonial administrative process led to a gradual, sometimes unconscious, transformation of traditional leaders into *de facto* collaborators. Subsequently, this involvement led to a diminution of their status in the eyes of their fellow Africans, many of whom felt betrayed by their leaders' co-option.

Nevertheless, these new responsibilities provided a means for acquiring a knowledge of how the colonial system worked and whether it might be used to benefit Africans. They facilitated the development of political and economic links with sympathetic Europeans who aided in the growth of educational and political institutions for Africans. And these new responsibilities enabled Africans, especially the traditional leaders, to share the wealth, however dispropor-

90

tionately, through government grants and salaries. Reliance upon African participation in the colonial administration meant that colonial governments had to train a minimum number of Africans for a variety of tasks. Largely because of their longer presence in the territories and because colonial governments sought to economize, Western missionary societies played the major role in this training. The number of schools were few and their distribution within each territory uneven. And in some regions, colonial governments actually discouraged the missions from establishing schools for fear they might offend certain groups' religious susceptibilities. Consequently, there were few if any Western-type schools in those areas. This was the case in the traditional Islamic states of northern Nigeria. In addition, the Western education which Africans did receive was directed towards a limited purpose: the missions wanted teachers, catechists and lay preachers, while the administration wanted clerks. Ironically, it was largely from this small group of Western-educated Africans that the core of the emergent nationalist élite appeared, which brings me to the paradoxical conclusion that by imparting Western education and values, colonialism laid the seed of its own destruction.

In almost every colonial African territory, discontent and the demand for self-government were embodied in a single mass political party. For the first time, enormous numbers of Africans were enlisted to oppose European rule in an organized, systematic manner. Trade unions, student groups, market mamas, ethnic associations and separatist churches became affiliated with the mass political party, uniting African groups into a single instrument in a campaign for independence.

A factor which contributed greatly to the growth and

success of the mass party was the weakening of the authority of traditional African leaders and the appearance of a new set of leaders. Colonial rule did not destroy the position of the African chiefs, although migration to the developing urban areas, the spread of Western ideas and education, as well as the chiefs' role as agents of colonial governments, did erode their traditional influence. The new nationalist leadership, deriving its power primarily from its status within the mass party, and the strength of the party within the colonial territory, could hardly establish itself as "the" voice of the people, until it had made progress towards displacing the older chiefly leadership. Until this was done, the emergent party leadership was liable to find itself labelled by colonial administrators as self-seeking, rabble-rousing usurpers not representative of the mass of African opinion.

Actually, the cards were well stacked against the chiefs. The colonial regimes tried to keep Africans loyal to their chiefly rulers, while at the same time developing the embryo of a modern export economy and imparting Western education. This contradictory policy did not work, and resulted in the further erosion of the powers of chiefs. For example, an African clerk, mine worker or war veteran could not be expected to pay attention to the dictates of tribal chiefs, while working in urban areas far from their tribal homes. Furthermore, men schooled by missionaries, who were adamant about freeing their pupils from so-called "heathen superstitions," were not likely to accept the claim of a chief to divine power or to an "in" with tribal gods, and, therefore, could not accept the chief's religious claims to authority.

The mass party, with its Western-educated leadership, came to represent the idea of the nation and national unity.

This feeling of national unity had to be built from scratch in territories composed of so many diverse groups which had been arbitrarily drawn together under colonial rule. Inevitably, the mass party and its leaders remained to rule, once the Empire was dismantled and self-government attained. But what remains when the Empire is gone? It had been comparatively simple to unite Africans against a system which their leaders considered anathema to human dignity. It was quite another matter to unite disparate groups into an integrated viable nation.

In order to illustrate the general direction Africa has taken since the Empire was dismantled and self-government embarked upon, I should like to return to a concept mentioned earlier in this lecture, in the context of one African country's experience. The concept is pluralism. The country is Uganda.

During the pre-colonial era, plural societies, that is, the incorporation of peoples with diverse historical, religious, ethnic and linguistic backgrounds under a single political system, were gradually—although not inevitably—evolving in sub-Saharan Africa. With the institution of colonialism, the gradual aspect of this evolution was replaced by forced pluralism. For with the institution of colonialism, peoples with quite different backgrounds were forced to live along side one another—but separately within their own distinct communities—sometimes racial, sometimes ethnic, sometimes religious and sometimes linguistic. They lived side by side, socially compartmentalized, but within the same colonial political system.

These colonial societies were not bound together by any cross-cutting loyalties or common values. Nor were these attributes—cross-cutting loyalties and common values—encouraged by the colonial powers. Divide and rule was the

93

guiding principle. And by pursuing that principle, exclusive communalism was not only perpetuated but exacerbated. Such societies were held together by dint of the force supplied by the colonial power. It follows then that, once independent, the future of plural societies becomes precarious.

When Uganda became independent, the power which held the society in check disappeared with the dissolution of the Empire. What remained was a society of non-integrated indigenous parts, on the one hand, and a society of non-integrated indigenous and non-indigenous parts, on the other. In the first category—the non-integrated indigenous components—only Africans were represented. In the second category Africans, Europeans and Asians were represented. In the first category, there were at least twenty different tribes speaking forty different languages. And although there was considerable mobility amongst these tribes, historically, there was little cultural contact, except in times of tribal wars.

Physical conditions had been instrumental in the distinctive development of these tribes with each or clusters of each developing a different type of social, political and economic organization in response to a particular environment. In the sparsely populated north the land was unfertile and poorly watered, with severe droughts being a not uncommon occurrence. This in a country where during the rainy season fourteen percent of the land becomes fragmented into swamps and marshes. But this occurs mainly in the south, not in the dry desolate north.

In response to environmental conditions, the north developed small, egalitarian, largely nomadic societies on land that could not sustain a sedentary economy, and a system of government which was decentralized and kinship oriented rather than centralized and hierarchically structured. The egalitarian and non-centralized nature of northern societies instilled in the peoples of these scattered tribes a strong sense of freedom, of non-comformity. Not only did they resist British colonial attempts at establishing formal political institutions, but after independence they resisted attempts of the new government to integrate the entire country by creating administrative districts incorporating the north. Ironically, the two national leaders of government that Uganda has had since it became independent in 1962—the deposed Milton Obote and the reigning military dictator, General Amin—came from the north.

The south is the antithesis of the north. It is densely populated. Its soil is amongst the most fertile in Africa. And it is blessed with bountiful rain. As its land was able to sustain a sedentary economy, stable stationary societies were created which evolved into four kingdoms: Buganda, Toro, Buryoro and Ankole. These kingdoms developed centralized systems of government which were hierarchically structured. Nineteenth-century explorers and missionaries were fascinated by them, but not always for the same reasons. Their culture, especially in Buganda, was amongst the most sophisticated to be found in the whole of Africa. It was in Buganda where the largest tribe in Uganda, the Baganda, resided. The Baganda of Buganda spoke Luganda! They had a king called the Kabaka, who had a prime minister, called the Katikkiro, who presided over the Kabaka's advisory council, the Lukiiko.

Living under these advanced and advantageous conditions, it is not surprising that the Baganda played a major role in the emergence of Uganda into self-government and modernity. Their kingdom became the center from which European political, social, and economic ideas spread or were imposed upon the rest of the country. They came to view themselves as an élite, apart. They were accused of cultural arrogance and were despised for its manifestations. Voraciously they absorbed the Western education which the north rejected. They converted to Christianity while the north remained Muslim. Their ethnic origin was Bantu, while the northerners were Nilo-Hamitics.

Consequently, as independence drew near, the attempt to unify the country actually meant an attempt to establish the supremacy of a central government over Buganda, which was no easy task as Buganda jealously guarded her uniquely favored position. After independence, one of the most critical problems of national integration has been that involving the well-advanced Baganda and the disadvantaged rest of the indigenous Uganda population. On the eve of independence, colonial administrators realized that Britain's policy in the dependency had reinforced and, in some instances, created obstacles for a united Uganda—obstacles such as entrenched tribalism, a scarcity of trained Africans in the civil service, and, in general, the absence of any sense of national loyalty.

Belatedly, the colonial government made attempts at containing tribalism, which previously it had not discouraged, in order to attain some sense of national consciousness and loyalty. Elected assemblies, earlier judged unsuitable for Africans, were created. And Africans were recruited for higher administrative positions, something which previously had never been considered. All of these attempts at integration were made at breakneck speed at the eleventh hour before independence. After independence the ill-prepared African government was forced to deal with the indigenous pluralism inherited from colonialism. At the same time, it had to solve new problems created by independence and modernity. Its inability to find the solution to the multitude of problems contributed to the rise of the military as an alternative to civilian government: a civilian government operated predominately by Bagandans; a military dominated by northerners.

In the second category of non-integrated parts making up Uganda's plural society were Africans, Europeans and Asians. Europeans in Uganda were never as significant in numbers nor in influence as they were in the neighboring colony of Kenya. With all arable land occupied and cultivated by Africans, European colonialists in Uganda were mainly engaged in managerial rather than homestead endeavors. There was no land for Asian cultivation either, but it was the presence of this group in Uganda which thrust the country into the forefront of international concern. Until 1947, Asians in East Africa who came from the Indian sub-continent were generally referred to as Indians. But with the creation of the separate states of India and Pakistan that expression was considered inappropriate and the term "Asian" has been used instead, although the use of Indian is not uncommon. Unlike others who form part of the so-called Indian Diaspora—such as the Asians in South Africa, Fiji, Mauritius, South America and the Caribbean— Asians in East Africa did not come as indentured laborers to work on lucrative European-owned sugar plantations. The majority came as coolies to do the manual labor required to build the Kenya-Uganda railway from Mombasa to Kampala at the turn of this century.

The Indian Diaspora is the result of an imperial policy pursued by the governments of the British Empire. India with her teeming millions was used as a source of cheap labor to stock plantations and public works projects in British colonies all over the world, especially in places where the indigenous inhabitants refused to do such work.

97

India was the brightest jewel in the British Empire's crown: its people could be deployed as cheap labor throughout the Empire, and the country could absorb the capital investments and manufactured goods from Britain. India's imperial importance caused Uganda to acquire also a place of prominence in the foreign policy of successive British governments.

Lake Victoria is the source of the White Nile. This river must flow through Uganda before it joins the Blue Nile—coming from Lake Tana in Ethiopia—at Khartoum in the Sudan and with it becomes the lifeline of Egypt. It was a primary objective of British imperial policy never to allow any country with the technical know-how of altering the course of rivers to gain sovereignty over lands through which the White Nile flowed. If such an event should occur, this could strike at the heart of Egypt which needed this water for its survival. Moreover, if such a power gained sovereignty, it might force Egypt to alter the arrangement under which the Suez Canal was operated, and under that arrangement, the deciding power was in the hands of the British.

Succinctly put, India was of primary importance because of its markets, investment potential and cheap labor. Egypt was of primary importance because the Suez Canal made the markets of India so accessible. And Uganda was of primary importance because the source of the Nile touched its borders.

Once the Kenya-Uganda railway was built, many Asians returned to India. Those who stayed and others who immigrated were encouraged to do so by the British. The British also encouraged them to enter business and trade rather than become agriculturalists. They prospered rapidly due to a lack of competition from the Africans, who did not have the expertise needed to operate a monetary commercial system.

Asians in East Africa are often applauded for being the purveyors of a money economy where previously a barter economy had existed. Little is said of how easy it was made for them. By 1920 a European-Asian partnership had evolved in which Europeans held political power and the Asians economic power. The Asians monopolized not only the commercial trades, but they acted as middlemen in the buying and selling of cotton, a product which was being developed as a lucrative cash crop. Many Asians exploited the Africans by overcharging "them" for "their" goods and services, while underpaying them for the fruits of African labor. As a consequence, Africans developed an attitude of hostility and distrust of Asians.

The colonial policy pursued by the British did much to exacerbate this attitude, as Asians were given preferential treatment over Africans. They were allowed elected representatives before the Africans received this right. On trains, ships, and in schools and hospitals, Asian accommodations were considerably better than those for Africans. These disparities led to the Asians' forgetting their own humble origins and assuming a behavior of superiority towards the Africans. Political events and independence happened too fast to allow a change in attitude by the Asians.

Even before independence, Asian wealth was obvious and universally resented by the Africans. After independence, hardly any Asian trusted the economic future of East Africa. Greater numbers than ever sent their money abroad, before the African governments put tight restrictions on the export of capital. This distrust of the economic future of African-governed East Africa was one of the main reasons, if not "the" reason, why Asians hesitated to take out East African citizenship when it was offered by African governments. They were afraid that they might not be able to join their foreign-housed money in an emergency, since the African governments might refuse to allow their new citizens to leave the country.

In the summer of 1972, General Amin, the President of Uganda, announced that all non-citizen Asians had to leave Uganda by November of 1972, and that all citizen Asians had to leave the towns and go and live in villages. He said that this decision was not based on racism but rather on the proposition that Uganda had to be developed for the benefit of the Africans. He accused the Asians of being economic saboteurs interested only in their own gains and not identifying with the common goals of the country. Amin's expulsion of Asians and his promise to put their business into African hands made him instantly popular with many Africans. That popularity may have diminished in recent months, as Amin has become more and more despotic, exhibiting those tyrannical tendencies so despised in his predecessor, Milton Obote. But then, national popularity has never been the source of Amin's political power. That source lies solely within the volatile and sometimes unruly Ugandan army.

The legacies of Empire are many, including the not inconsequential opening of the African mind to new ideas and concepts for coping with the environment in order to live a longer, healthier and, hopefully, happier life. But the major continental problem is how to integrate the diverse parts in each country into a viable nation. For in the aftermath of Empire, of which Uganda is a microcosm of plural societies found all over Africa, there exists a continent fragmented by tribal, religious and cultural cleavages.

Throughout the continent the most pressing and challenging task lies squarely in the domestic realm—that of developing some degree of internal cohesion and consensus. In pursuit of these ends it might prove beneficial if the participants in this nation-building process learned to *forget* some of the myth and reality of their past history. Not an easy task in a developing nation such as Uganda; not an easy task in a developed nation such as the United States of America.

Walter Morris-Hale

AFTERMATH OF EMPIRE

AFTERMATH OF EMPIRE

INTRODUCTION

"TIMELY and timeless," said President Mendenhall in his opening remarks on Wednesday, characterizing the theme of this session of the Alumnae College. A theme close to the interests of Hans Kohn, citizen of the world whose first loyalty was to humankind; who taught many generations of students, at Smith and elsewhere, denouncing the evils of nationalism, parent of imperialistic drives. A theme close, too, to the interests of Vera Brown Holmes who in her courses on imperialism and on the history of the Americas, and in her writings, has made students (now alumnae) and readers aware of the somber aspects of imperialistic greed.

Hatred and Admiration

Many, perhaps most, have a somewhat ambivalent attitude towards imperialism. It is damned, and at the same time admired. "Down with imperialism! down with imperialists!" is a loud, at times a deafening, cry rising from the masses of the world intelligentsia—the fast expanding, dynamic and emotional minority now pushing and pulling humankind along its perilous course. But whatever their attitude toward present-day events, when it comes to lecturing in colleges and universities, to writing books and articles, lecturers and authors praise Empires and exalt Empire builders.[1]

Republicans Cicero and Cato, whose success would have caused the disruption of the Roman Empire, are contemptuously dismissed in a few words; Caesar and Augustus, who destroyed the republic and saved the Empire, receive panegyrics. The attempt of Athenians and other ancient

1. Here are a few random expressions of admiration:

During the *Pax Mongolica* "a girl with a pot of gold on her head could walk alone and unharmed from end to end of the Mongol lands. . . . As military impact mellowed into imperial relations, had come distinguished men . . . Chinese scholars, Persian astronomers, Indian philosophers and mathematicians. More important, long-distance trade burgeoned under the Mongol Peace. . . . A Eurasian world market was emerging." (Stuart Legg, *The Heartland* [New York: Capricorn Books, 1970], p. 304.)

"The establishment of the Sokoto caliphate . . . united the Hausa states politically for the first time in their history. . . . It brought . . . renewed vigour . . . to Bornu. . . . [It gave] stimulus to learning, education and the spread of Islam. . . . Great libraries grew up at Sokoto and Segu; literacy became necessary for high office. . . . Internally there was a considerable degree of peace, order and good government which encouraged trade. Farmers could till the soil, herdsmen tend their cattle, artisans and merchants ply their trade." (J. B. Webster and A. A. Boahen, *History of West Africa* [New York: Praeger, 1970], pp. 14–15.)

"Think of a whole continent assimilated to a European civilization and life . . . ; of an absorption into the ways of Europe . . . as early as the sixteenth century, the Indies had already contributed to our Atlantic world a school of painting . . . and a dance . . . which Bach thought worthy of its music. . . ." (Salvador de Madariaga, *The Rise of the Spanish American Empire* [New York: The Free Press, 1947], p. 334).

The world "Europeans have helped to create . . . is a world in which the drama of life has been shifted . . . from a tribal to a national and from a national to a world stage . . . in which the common material lot has been improved . . . in which the force of death has been weakened and pain dulled . . . of growing law and order . . . of growing enlightenment." (William Woodruff, *Impact of Western Man: A Study in Europe's Role in World Economy 1750–1960* [New York: St. Martin's Press, 1967], pp. 335f.)

Greeks to create a democratic way of life is damned for "its insane and pitiless wars . . . its lack of moral restraint, its corrupt individualism, its . . . failure to [achieve] order and peace"[2] while Alexander, called the Great, is showered with praises. The liberals among French 1789ers and their successors—including Madame Roland and Madame de Staël—who wanted free institutions which act as brakes to imperialistic drives, are looked down on with disdain, while Napoleon, conqueror and slaughterer on the scale of Caesar and Alexander, is celebrated and his deeds glorified. Today it is fashionable for anti-imperialists, while exalting or excusing or justifying Uncle Joe who emulated Ivan IV, his successors who consolidated the Empire, and the Chairman who emulated Wu Ti,[3] to throw mud at those who, committed to democracy, a generation ago fought wars that caused Empires to collapse, and later contained—successfully for two decades—other dynamic Empires.

Empires fascinate even when imperialism is condemned; the imperialism of others of course, not one's own—as for instance when former French subjects now bent on subjugating their neighbors condemn French imperialism, or when national communists enthusiastic about the imperial exploits of Stalin condemn capitalist imperialism. There is nothing strange in this contradiction, one more expression of the irrational which rules most minds and which tragi-

2. Will Durant, *The Life of Greece* (New York: Simon and Schuster, 1939), p. 671.

3. In years to come there may be other revisionists who will write contemptuously of Bruening and Braun who in a fumbling way tried to uphold democracy, and of Amendola and Hamaguchi who gave their lives for it; they will celebrate the feats of German Fuehrer and Air Marshal, of the Italian Duce, of Japanese generals, and bewail their failure to maintain Empires. Revisionism expresses sympathy for the Soviet system and the Soviet way of life.

cally is gaining ground. Imperial expansion is resisted, but once an Empire has been consolidated, and has lasted long enough, it numbers among its supporters descendants of the conquered peoples as well as descendants of the conqueror. It brings order, it brings peace, it brings splendid monuments: what else does one want?[4]

Definition

What imperialism is can be said in a few words: *the rule of a people over other peoples who do not want to be ruled.* The last seven words are as important as the first eight. There are instances of peoples surrendering their sovereignty of their own free will in order to be protected, or to be allowed to merge with a more advanced, more prosperous, more powerful people, from ancient Bithynians in 74 B.C. to medieval Icelanders in 1264, to Cambodians in 1863, to millions of Europeans who would prefer to be sovietized

---

4. "Citizens [of universal states] . . . are apt not only to desire with their whole hearts that this earthly commonwealth of theirs may live for ever, but actually to believe that the immortality of this human institution is assured. . . . In the history of the Roman Empire, which was the universal state of the Hellenic world, we find the generation that had witnessed the establishment of the *Pax Augusta* asserting . . . that the Empire and the City that built it have been endowed with a common immortality. . . . A Greek man of letters . . . was praying that a fugitive October might be miraculously transformed into a perpetual June. 'Let us evoke the gods and all the children of the gods, and let us pray them to grant this empire and this city life and prosperity world without end. May they endure until ingots learn to float on the sea and until trees forget to blossom in the spring. And long . . . the supreme magistrate and his children . . . be with us to carry on their work of dispensing happiness to all their subjects.' " (Arnold J. Toynbee, *A Study of History* [London: Oxford Univ. Press, 1954], VII, 7–10.)

and fewer millions who would prefer to be Americanized, and to individuals everywhere.[5]

It makes no difference whether the people who do not want to be ruled are in the same state as the rulers, as is the case of Kashmiris in India; or outside,[6] as is the case of Angolan Bantus; or whether they are a majority, like Andean Indians in several South American republics, or a minority like Berbers in the Maghreb: imperialism is rule over unwilling peoples.

Awareness of Imperialism

Awareness of imperialism and the widespread antagonism particularly against its Western brand, are recent phenomena, partly—or perhaps largely—the result of more abundant information than was ever available in the past, of freer discussion than there has ever been,[7] in short, the result of democratic liberties. However, imperialism has since time immemorial been a major phenomenon in the history and

5. "In 1937 . . . Senghor explained that solidarity between Africa and France was a necessity because: 'We are engaged in the same destiny. There are for us formidable competitors in economic battles, as well as in political competition. If we wish to survive, the necessity of an adaptation, of an assimilation, cannot escape us. Our *milieu* is no longer only West-African, it is also French, it is international; it is Afró-French.' " (I. L. Markowitz, *Léopold Sédar Senghor and the Politics of Négritude* [New York: Atheneum, 1969], p. 81.)

6. Imperialism is "the policy of a state aiming at establishing control beyond its borders over people unwilling to accept such control," says the *Encyclopædia Britannica* (Chicago: Benton, 1964), xii, 121. The rule of Chinese over millions of Turks, Chuangs, Mongols, Manchus, Tibetans, etc., is imperialism, as is the rule of Portuguese over millions of Bantus.

7. "Hostility . . . derives . . . from the actual flow of world news. . . ." (C. C. O'Brien in "Contemporary Forms of Imperialism" in *Studies on the Left*, vi, No. 4 [1965], quoted in R. A. Austin, ed., *Modern Imperialism, Western Overseas Expansion and Its Aftermath 1776–1965* [Lexington, Mass.: D. C. Heath & Co., 1969], p. 188.)

prehistory of the human race. There has been no lack of sophisticated and sugared justifications in the remote[8] and recent[9] past, and there is no lack today, but imperialism remains the manifestation of primitiveness, of the sordid, greedy and cruel struggle waged by the strong against the weak, to dislodge them so as to possess their lands and their resources, to destroy them or to make them untouchables,

8. The establishment of order and the enforcement of discipline is the justification for conquest, according to Jules Harmand, quoted in Philip D. Curtin, *Imperialism* (New York: Harper & Row, 1971), p. 300.

"It was the Europe of the eighteenth and nineteenth centuries, of general ideas, of the ideas of progress and the rights of man, of scientific discovery and mechanical invention, of dynamism and restless change, which was to move India. . . . Of course there was colonialism . . . imperialism . . . exploitation. . . . A regime which was exclusively colonialist or imperialist would have left an India exhausted or resentful or both. Instead of this we have seen an India full of life, energy, and hope, carrying on in many respects with remarkable continuity," wrote admiringly Percival Spear. (*India: A Modern History* [Ann Arbor: Univ. of Michigan Press, 1961], p. 451.)

The seventh-century Indian conqueror "Harsha had realized the weakness of a cluster of small kingdoms and had decided to conquer his neighbours to weld them into an imperial structure." (Romila Thapar, *A History of India* [London: Penguin Books, 1966], p. 144.)

And in China, centuries ago "many political theorists anxiously pointed out that only under a unified, centralized state could peace and order prevail, and they saw no alternative to a bureaucratic autocratic rule." (Dun J. Li, *The Ageless Chinese* [New York: Scribner's Sons, 1965], p. 100.)

9. Imperialism is "the informing spirit, the unseen force from within the race itself, which in the past has shapen and in the present continues to shape this . . . material frame of empire." (J. A. Cramb, *The Origins and Destiny of Imperial Britain* [London: Murray, 1915], p. 5.)

"Colonization must go on as before . . . by . . . unilateral action, resulting in the expropriation, enslavement, and even extermination of the uncivilized." (G. B. Shaw in letter to *The Times* of London, October 12, 1935, supporting Italian Fascist imperialism in East Africa.)

Helots, serfs, slaves. Imperialism kills people. It also kills ways of life—the Christian way in North Africa and, later, the Islamic in Spain, the democratic way in Czechoslovakia and the Lamaist in Tibet in recent decades. To kill a way of life is to kill the soul of nations, which for centuries Turks did to Balkan peoples, and Spaniards to American Indians.

Universality of Imperialism

To be correctly understood, the imperial phenomenon has to be seen in its total context: not this or that Empire, not this or that conqueror, but as a structure, a way of organizing society. Understanding thus moves from the particular and ephemeral to the institutional and lasting. Forty-five centuries have intervened between the Akkadian subjugation of neighboring communities and the Soviet conquests. Of what had been done earlier, and of what was done by peoples who left no record of their deeds—except at times in myths and legends—there is an inkling even when data are lacking: thus the obliteration of most aborigines by Malayans in western Pacific archipelagoes, of most Bushmen by Negroes in tropical Africa, the subjugation of Dravidians by Aryans in India, of Zapotecans and other peoples by Toltecs in the Mexican highlands.

Imperialism is old, even if Empires belong to that later period called civilization when institutions are created for the enactment and enforcement of laws, the state comes into existence, religion is organized, urban centers are built, and commerce and industry develop. Besides being old, imperialism is universal. Why, but why? all ask.

111

Imperialism is universal because of man's nature, many say; because of his "warlike instincts,"[10] according to some; because of greed for material things,[11] according to others obediently following fashionable ways of thinking; because so wills God or any god invented in recent generations by the free-flowing imagination of thinkers taking full advantage of greater freedom of expression than had ever existed —the gods known as the Spirit of the Times, the Class Struggle, the Survival of the Fittest; because of changes in climate, sudden increases in population, the invention of this or that; because some are born superior to others; or because of something else.

The field of the why is an open one: certainty eludes us; it is a field of shifting sands. What is known is how Empires are created, and in the "how" one may find the "why." "War," many contend, "is the father of all things."[12] This is an exaggeration; but expansion, through conquest, occupation or concession, either limited or "conceived as an

10. According to Schumpeter "warlike instincts" and "structural elements and organizational forms oriented toward war" are "precapitalist elements in our social life" to which "more weight must be given in every concrete case of imperialism than to export monopolist interests. . . ." (Joseph Schumpeter, *Imperialism, Social Classes* [New York: Meridian Books, 1955], p. 98.)

11. "Three . . . varieties [of empires] have been distinguished, namely (I) the original, servile, empires based upon slave labour, (II) the mercantile empires based upon the plundering sort of commerce . . . of the East India Company's eighteenth-century empire in India, and (III) the fully developed capitalist empires. . . ." (John Strachey, *The End of Empire* [New York: Random House, 1960], p. 325.) For Strachey and like-minded dialectical materialists, Empires—from the Persian in the sixth century B.C. to the Soviet in the twentieth century—not based on slavery, commerce and capitalism evidently did not and do not exist.

12. Quoted in Toynbee, *A Study of History*, v (1935), 15.

endless process in which every country would serve only as stepping stone for further expansion,"[13] is the product of nothing more complicated than might, usually in its crudest manifestation, military power, and sometimes, more rarely, in more complex and subtle manifestations such as cultural superiority and economic pressure. As in all human things, there are exceptions, but imperialism basically has no other source than the fact of physical, i.e., military, strength.[14]

13. Hannah Arendt, *The Origins of Totalitarianism* (New York: Meridian Books, 1967), p. 215.

14. Inclusive of this century's enduring Soviet Empire and the short-lived Empires of Germany and Japan in the 1930's and early 40's, most Empires have been created by dynamic rulers of militarily strong states. Not having to contend with internal opposition, commanding efficient armed forces, rulers from Sargon to Stalin expanded the states they controlled until they met the obstacle of a force equivalent to their own—anything from a physical barrier (ocean, desert, mountain range) to a state with a strong army.

In the modern era, absolute power and military superiority created or enlarged the Mogul, Ottoman, Portuguese and Spanish Empires of the sixteenth century; the Russian Empire which grew erratically from 1552 to 1886, and its successor, the Soviet Empire, which extended further in 1939–1948; French overseas Empires and the Napoleonic one in Europe; the short-lived Persian Empire and the further expansion of the Chinese Empire in the eighteenth century; several ephemeral Empires in Africa in the nineteenth, from that of the Zulus south of the Zambesi to the Egyptian one under Mohammed Ali, to that of the Fulani in the Sudan. These were conventional Empires like those of ancient Persians, the Hans in China, the Indian Guptas, Alexander the Great and Genghis Khan.

There were instances when expansion through state action carried out the freely expressed will of citizens. This created the Athenian Empire of the fifth century B.C., which soon crashed, bringing Athens down with it; also the equally short-lived Empires of medieval Italian maritime republics such as Pisa; and the enduring Empire conquered by Romans in the third and second centuries B.C., which was a major element in the collapse of republican institutions.

In a different category are the few Empires created or expanded since the seventeenth century at least partially through initiatives

113

Evidence shows that force in one way or another creates Empires. But why use force? Simply because between states (or any other kinds of independent communities) there is anarchy, and where there is anarchy force regulates relationships. Anarchy is implicit in the adjective "sovereign" used as an attribute of the word "state": the adjective means that on one hand the state is the source of law, and on the other that there is no law above the state. States make agreements among themselves and at times even abide by them but, whatever the motive, the abiding comes from an

---

taken by citizens acting in a private capacity. From around 1620, Dutch adventurers, traders and planters presented the United Provinces with an Empire that had losses and gains but most of which was consolidated between 1818 and 1910 as the Dutch East Indies (now Indonesia), by the government of the Netherlands. Adventurers, traders and planters, plus several tens of thousands of religious and political dissenters in the seventeenth century (and, even if on a small scale, from the 1780's on for about a hundred years, abolitionists, missionaries and other humanitarians) presented Great Britain with an Empire which was further expanded by state action; in consequence, half a century ago one-quarter of the world's land area was ruled by English-speaking nations. The activities of an international group with headquarters in Brussels, and of a few Germans, precipitated the partition of tribal Africa in the mid-1880's. Americans who moved into territories nominally Spanish or Mexican, and later into Pacific islands, paved the way for the annexation by the United States of the Floridas, over half of Mexico, and Hawaii. Imbalance of forces in the anarchic international situation was also the source of this type of imperial expansion: here, however, the action of citizens in their private capacity replaced state action, or at any rate preceded it. Instead of conquerors like Suleiman the Magnificent, Ivan the Terrible, Nadir Shah, Napoleon, Chaka; instead of the generals and admirals of Charles V, Mohammed Ali, the Meiji Emperor Mutsuhito, the generals of Ch'en Lung, Nicolas I, Hajj Omar, there were small, even tiny, private groups, from the English Plymouth Company of the early seventeenth century to the German Colonization Society nearly three hundred years later.

114

inner decision. It does not derive from an authority higher than that of the state, which enforces respect for agreements. Without an enforcing agency, ancient jurists taught, there is no law, and if there is no law there is anarchy. Anarchy is what has always existed on the international scene and exists today in the world community of seven and a half score sovereign states.

Military Might

Political scientists list the elements making for the might of a state. Some of them can be measured,[15] most cannot: national cohesion, morale of the citizens, efficiency of the institutions, discipline, character, leadership, the energy[16] which varies from community to community, and in the same community varies in time. Might may ultimately be nothing more than physical courage and moral commitment. In many cases it is simply a more efficient armed force, a more efficient weapon: phalanxes and legions in the ancient Mediterranean world; Mongol and French caval-

15. Among others: size, population, economic resources, numbers and equipment of the military establishment.

16. "When the floodgates of Europe's creative energy were opened . . . there grew within Europe industrial and manufacturing power greater than the world had known before." (William Woodruff, *Impact of Western Man*, p. 2.)

A surge of energy favors expansion, a decline of energy produces weakness: "A great deal of national energy" among Greeks "was a major factor in the subjugation by Romans of Greece and the Hellenistic Middle East." (Theodor Mommsen, *The History of Rome* [New York: Philosophical Library, 1959], p. 181.)

"When we reflect upon the vices of these bandits [the Vikings] or recoil from their cruel deeds, we must also remember the discipline, the fortitude, the comradeship and martial virtues which made them the most formidable and daring race in the world." (Winston Spencer Churchill, *A History of the English-Speaking Peoples* [New York: Dodd, Mead, 1958], I, 94.)

ries later; the Spanish infantry in the sixteenth century, the British navy in the eighteenth, German and Soviet armored divisions in the twentieth were all efficient machines which carried forth conquerors along imperial roads;[17] from javelin to H-bomb, a new weapon could ensure military superiority.

Conventional Empires

There have been scores of Empires, enough to draw conclusions about their nature. Superior force makes them; in all but a few (about which more later) force keeps them going;[18] ruled despotically by a despotic state, they are struc-

17. The Romans' "military system, their levies, arms, exercises, subordination, marches, encampments, and the invincible legion" led "the arms of the republic, sometimes vanquished in battle, always victorious in war . . . to the Euphrates, the Danube, the Rhine, and the ocean." (Edward Gibbon, *The Decline and Fall of the Roman Empire*, D. A. Saunders, ed. [New York: The Viking Press, 1962], pp. 620f.)

"The first systematic 'opening and development' of Ling-nan [South China] began with the dispatch by the Ch'en Emperor in B.C. 234 of an army . . . to capture the Lu-liang territory. . . . The half-million men he dispatched were divided up into five armies. . . . Ch'in Shih Huang commanded the forced transplantation of some half a million military agricultural colonists to the Wu Ling . . . region." (Harold J. Wiens, *China's March toward the Tropics* [Hamden, Conn.; The Shoe String Press, 1954], pp. 132f.)

In Asia, in the period 1850–1914 "there was no protection of any sort against the superior *military* power of the imperialists." (Michael Edwardes, *The West in Asia 1850–1915: A Concise Survey History of Imperialism and Its Effects* [New York: Capricorn Books, 1967], p. 207.)

"The army . . . becomes the arbiter [and] sooner or later it will realize its power and will hold over the government's head the threat of a manifesto." (Frantz Fanon, *The Wretched of the Earth* [London: Penguin Books, 1967], p. 140.)

18. "An imperial structure requires two essentials: a well organized administration and the political loyalty of the subjects," wrote the Asian historian Thapar (*A History of India*, p. 89), echoed by a

turally the same in all continents and at all times. From the Chinese Empire thousands of years ago to the Soviet one in 1973, they belong to the mainstream of human development. Because of similarities in origin, structure and results, they form a conventional type. Whatever the outcome of an enduring Empire—continuing subjugation of subject peoples or their enforced assimilation[19]—imperialism has meant cruelty.[20] Hans slaughtered the peoples of South China; Caesar's soldiers may have massacred as much as one-third of the people of Gaul; in one short-lived nineteenth-century Sudanese Empire, survivors were one-fourth of the original population, and in another, one-fifth. "Slaughter" and "massacre" are words; percentages are

---

Western socialist: "An empire has to be administered, and the administration must be military and bureaucratic. . . . It must also display a minimum of efficiency." (George Lichtheim, *Imperialism* [New York: Praeger, 1971], p. 21.)

19. Chou En-lai complained: "Our voices have been suppressed, our aspirations shattered, and our destiny placed in the hands of others." (Chou En-lai, in 1955, quoted in P. E. Sigmund, Jr., ed., *The Ideologies of the Developing Nations* [New York: Praeger, 1963], p. 51.) But this is what the Chinese did to the peoples they had conquered, and are likely to do to those they will conquer: "The Han-Chinese merely absorbed the aborigines into Han culture." (Wiens, *China's March toward the Tropics*, p. 334.)

20. "The new empire [of Delhi sultans] . . . began as an army of occupation. . . . Turks possessed the faculty of united action as well as of daring leadership. Because of the paucity of their numbers they resorted to terror tactics. . . . Because of their lack of sophistication they gave a fanatical twist to Islam. . . . Their rule was a military occupation on a religious and racial foundation." (Percival Spear, *India: A Modern History* [Ann Arbor: The Univ. of Michigan Press, 1961], p. 105.)

"The price of unification [under Ch'in Shih Huang-ti, Emp. 247–207] was a heavy one: millions of lives had been lost and much property destroyed or damaged, not to mention the moral degeneration that resulted from an almost continuous state of war." (Dun J. Li, *The Ageless Chinese*, p. 99.)

117

statistical items: agonies and immense suffering give meaning and life to words and items. The success of imperialism is measured by the extent to which ideas and values making bondage a way of life are accepted, as happened in China,[21] as happened for several centuries in Spain's overseas possessions.

Stagnation

All Empires formed before modern times have collapsed, excepting one, the Chinese. If one wants to have an idea of what humankind will be if a future world state is the outcome of a triumphant imperialistic drive, one should look at what China had been for over twenty centuries until, after several decades of unrelenting Western pressures, it was torn apart two generations ago; at what China is, now that the greatest nation on earth is recuperating from the turmoil and disruption of the first half of the century. Of Empires formed in modern times only two survive, the shaky Portuguese one and the Russian, the latter efficiently restructured half a century ago as the Soviet Empire. All enduring Empires—those that survived their founder or renovator and lasted several generations—are characterized by stagnation sooner or later.

At first, the concentration of arbitrary power organizing and mobilizing resources has often made for golden ages, celebrated by historians, philosophers, poets. But the same

21. "Chinese humanism emphasized man's relationship with other men rather than man as an independent, free individual. While Renaissance humanism freed man from his bondage to other men . . . Chinese humanism . . . strengthened that bondage. Chinese philosophers . . . were not interested in establishing a society composed of equal, independent individuals, but a society where man's position was clearly and carefully prescribed." (Dun J. Li, *The Ageless Chinese*, p. 67.) This is a sample of the way of thinking which made Chinese the peoples conquered by China.

concentration, being achieved at the expense of individual autonomy—the source of all creativity—produces the succeeding silver and bronze ages, and eventually leads to stagnation.[22]

Utopias and Empires

Current (often spurious) anti-imperialism should not blind us to the appeal the Empires have. Empire means unity. After resistance stemming from an autonomous past has been overcome in the course of generations, the blessings of unity compensate for shortcomings and defects. For

22. "The vast despotism of the Caesars, gradually effacing all natural peculiarities and assimilating the remotest provinces of the empire to each other, augmented the evil [narrowness and sameness of thought, barrenness and degeneracy]. At the close of the third century after Christ the prospects of [Western] mankind were fearfully dreary. . . . That great community was then in danger of experiencing a calamity far more terrible than any of the quick, inflammatory, destroying maladies to which nations are liable—a tottering, drivelling, paralytic longevity, the immortality of the Struldbrugs, a Chinese civilization. It would be easy to indicate many points of resemblance between the subjects of Diocletian and the people of that Celestial Empire where, during many centuries, nothing has been learned or unlearned; where government, where education, where the whole system of life, is a ceremony; where knowledge forgets to increase and multiply, and . . . experiences neither waste nor augmentation." (Macaulay, Lord: "History" in T. B. Macaulay, *Miscellaneous Writings* [London: Longmans, Green, 1860], I, 263f.)

In relation to seventeenth-century Persia "the Safavid empire collapsed. . . . The culture continued to be precious and delightful . . . but its aggressive quality and infectious nature had passed away." And to eighteenth-century India: "The [Moghul] empire had ceased to exercise . . . that charm which draws men to causes and people by the infectious magic of its qualities." (Percival Spear, *India*, pp. 173, 174.)

Long before in India "with . . . the emphasis on older texts, formal education tended to become a repetition of statements rather than a questioning of facts in an attempt to obtain further elucidation. . . . The result was intellectual inbreeding." (Thapar, *A History of India*, p. 254.)

most—too many for the good of democracy—unity is bliss because it means absence of dissent, of opposition, of anything different in what matters most and causes most tensions: ideas and values.

Few are the heretics convinced that factionalism, tensions and other unwelcome consequences of individual liberty— the free rein given to spontaneity within the range compatible with the requirements of the social order—are preferable to the quiet, docility and conformity which the authorities maintain by eliminating dissidents and deviationists in the properly organized and properly integrated society.

Utopias are less utopian than the word indicates.[23] They share the common feature of aspiration toward a static order. Even when not envisaging a universal state, they ignore diversity in things of the mind and postulate identical conformist communities. Utopias represent the ideal toward which Empires strive. Ancient Egyptians, who lived for a longer time than any other civilized community in a static order, came close to realization of the ideal. Whatever

23. "The Utopias . . . are really programmes of action . . . and the action which they intended to evoke is the 'pegging,' at a certain social level, of an actual society which . . . has entered upon a decline that must end in a fall unless the downward movement can be artificially arrested. . . . In almost all Utopias . . . an invincible stable equilibrium is the supreme social aim to which all other social values are subordinated and, if need be, sacrificed. This is true of the Hellenic Utopias. . . . Their negative inspiration is a profound hostility to Athenian democracy. . . . The programme of *Brave New World* . . . is to 'peg' . . . Western Society at the level of the Industrial System. . . . The application of . . . Western Physical Science to practical life is to be carried to extremes, and at the same time the vast increase in the material 'drive' behind all our actions is to be counteracted and rendered innocuous by converting the spiritual voltage of Human Nature from high to low tension." (Toynbee, *A Study of History*, III, 89f, 100f.)

the rhetoric, contemporary communalists pursue the same goal. At the practical level of everyday activities, most human beings want to realize as much of utopia as possible, want a strong authority committed to the enforcement of conformity.

Progress Requires the End of Empires

Hated while in the process of formation, Empires have been praised[24] by later generations who lamented their passing as a major disaster. It has never been a disaster. Excepting the few Empires held by democratic imperial powers, Empires are dead ends. Whatever the turmoil and the suffering when an Empire disintegrates, its end destroys a stumbling block, opens the road to new experience—not necessarily to progress but at least to a possibility for it.[25]

24. "In the Sudan . . . peace and security reigned everywhere in all the provinces [of the Songhay empire] . . . from the frontiers of the land of Dendi to the fractions of the land of Al-Hamdiyya, and from the countries of the land of Bonduku to Taghaza and Tawat, as well as in the dependencies of those countries." (Abd-al-Rahman, "Songhay and the Moroccan Invasion," in R. O. Collins, ed., *African History: Text and Readings* [New York: Random House, 1971], p. 36.)

25. The two passages quoted concern creativity in non-imperial ages:

"The five centuries after 771 B.C. were a period of paradoxes. On the one hand it was marked with incessant warfare, political anarchy, and moral degeneration. On the other hand, it was an era of dynamic social and economic changes and of great masters of new ideas. In fact, from the point of view of ideology, there has never been a period so constructive." (Dun J. Li, *The Ageless Chinese*, p. 66.)

"The period from the eighth to the thirteenth centuries is sometimes referred to as the 'dark ages,' when classical Hindu culture declined and political disintegration facilitated the conquest of the sub-continent by a totally foreign power. But, far from being a dark period, it is a formative period . . . since many institutions of present-day India began to take enduring shape during this period." (Thapar, *A History of India*, p. 89.)

Violence Ends Empires

Except for the few Empires held by heretical nations founded on liberty (and because of that, short-lived), Empires which have survived their founders have collapsed under the impact of external forces or, less euphemistically, wars successfully waged by invaders. It would be tedious to list examples taken from all phases of historical development in all continents. Invaders from the east ended the Akkadian. Sheer weight of steel ended half a dozen old and new Empires in the twentieth century. Wars may cease (actually, as things are now, this is likely for major wars): this would mean that whatever Empire now exists will go on existing. One day there may be a universal state embracing the planet: if sustained as Empires have always been, by force, it will last forever and progress will cease.

There is much to admire in Empires, but anyone committed to the idea of progress—for some a better life, for others the duty to develop to the utmost the abilities and capabilities with which human beings are endowed (and of which, scientists tell us, only a fraction has thus far been used)—is grateful that Empires have ended, that in the West and in the Middle East humanity has been spared the fate that befell the noblest nation of all, the Chinese. Because of their authoritarian structure, enduring Empires, however brightened by magnificent and efficient (and at times also benevolent) rulers, by Asokha, Marcus Aurelius, Haüan Tsung, Huayna Capac, are dead ends, graves in which human creativity lies buried.

Aftermath

The outcome of violence, the collapse of conventional Empires means tragedy. Noble buildings and useful artifacts

122

become ruins. People die. Survivors suffer.[26] The galloping of the Four Horsemen[27] marks the end of Empire, the Assyrian twenty-six centuries ago, the Japanese twenty-eight years ago. Imposing institutional structures break up.[28]

26. "From distant Maeotis, the icy Don, the savage Massagetes . . . hordes of Huns had swept through and were spreading slaughter and terror in all directions. . . . These savages . . . spared neither religion nor dignity nor age. The wails of infants roused no pity." (St. Jerome, quoted in Moses Hadas, *A History of Rome from Its Origins to 529 A.D. as Told by the Roman Historians* [Garden City, N.Y.: Doubleday, 1956], pp. 224f.)

27. "See how swiftly death comes upon the world," wrote the Roman poet Orientius, "and how many peoples the violence of war has stricken. . . . Some lay as food for the dogs; others were killed by the flames that licked their homes. In the villages and country houses, in the fields and the countryside, on every road—death, sorrow, slaughter, fires and lamentations" followed in the wake of the barbarians' crossing of the Rhine on December 31, 406. (Gerald Simons, *Barbarian Europe* [New York: Time-Life Books, 1968], p. 20.)

As the result of the disruption of the Empire of Songhay "everything changed. . . . Danger took the place of security, misery replaced opulence, and trouble, calamity, and violence succeeded tranquility. People destroyed each other on all sides, in all places, and in all directions. There was rapine and war. Neither life nor goods nor the condition of the inhabitants was spared." (Abd-al-Rahman, "Songhay and the Moroccan Invasion," in Collins, ed., *African History*, p. 36.)

"In the twenty turbulent years [after 1817] . . . almost every major city of the [Oya] empire had been sacked. Farming was difficult and famine and disease swept the land. Armies pillaged everything of value and carried hundreds into slavery. Each new defeat . . . sent waves of refugees. . . ." (Webster and Boahen, *A History of West Africa*, p. 91.)

28. "Tokhtamish's . . . conflict with Timur . . . loosened the bonds of political allegiance which held its [the Golden Horde's] vassals in check. . . . The collapse of the Horde led to a situation not unlike that which had prevailed before 633/1236. Throughout the steppelands . . . roamed . . . semi-independent Turkish nomads. . . . In certain favoured areas settled agricultural and commercial life continued, and these areas became the centres of political units. . . ." (M. E. Yapp, "The Golden Horde and Its Successors," in Holt, Lambton,

123

Fragmentation is a major result of the end of Empire, the fragments usually being inferior to the whole in all respects. There are still extant more than twenty successor states of the Ottoman Empire, and of the Spanish over twenty in both hemispheres. Twenty successor states could be identified in 1918 shortly after the Tsarist Empire had broken up, and more than twenty when the Third Reich disintegrated in 1945 under the weight of Allied steel. It is a meager consolation that at times fragmentation facilitates the diffusion of civilization,[29] as happened in the third century B.C. in the Middle East, or prepares the ground for the coming of a higher civilization later.[30] Sometimes, either foreigners or a formerly discriminated against section of the population quickly restructures the Empire, perhaps on a higher cultural level (as when the Hellenized Macedonian Empire replaced the Persian) or perhaps on a lower level (as when

---

Lewis, eds., *The Cambridge History of Islam* [Cambridge: University Press, 1970], I, 498.)

"Then civil war and faction descended on the court and the provinces rapidly dropped away. . . . The time was known as the Great Anarchy or . . . the Time of Troubles." (Spear, *India: A Modern History*, p. 180.)

29. "Hellenistic Greece did not feel Alexander's death as the 'end of an age': it looked upon him as the beginning of 'modern' times. . . . Greek civilization . . . conquered new areas and spread in three directions. . . . The Greeks moved by hundreds of thousands into Asia and Egypt, Epirus and Maudon; and not only did Ionia flower again, but Hellenic blood, language, and culture made its way into the interior of Asia Minor, into Phoenicia and Palestine, through Syria and Babylonia . . . even to Bactria and India. Never had the Greek spirit shown more zest and courage; never had Greek letters and arts won so wide a victory." (Durant, *The Life of Greece*, p. 557.)

30. The Mongol Empire "within sixty years . . . had become a hollow husk. . . . It left behind the seeds of an infinitely wider and deeper revolution. . . . It set Europe on the road to an era of world domination that was to last until the Second World War." (Legg, *The Heartland*, p. 319.)

Mongols briefly superseded Chinese and Iranians), or on the same level, as when the Soviet Empire replaced the Tsarist in Russia. Our imaginations are struck by the cases with which we are most familiar, those in which a Dark Age[31] followed the end of Empire, the end of the Mauryan, the Roman, the Arab Empires.

31. "In the last days of Pope Eugenius the Fourth . . . the learned Poggio and a friend ascended the Capitoline hill. . . . The place and the object gave ample scope for moralizing on the vicissitudes of fortune, which spares neither man nor the proudest of his works, which buries empires and cities in a common grave; and it was agreed that, in proportion to her former greatness, the fall of Rome was the more awful and deplorable." (Gibbon, *The Decline and Fall of the Roman Empire*, p. 685.)

"Saint Jerome . . . was devoted to the service of a Church that avowedly placed its hopes in the Commonwealth of God . . . ; yet this news [of the fall of Rome in 410] . . . affected Jerome so profoundly that for the moment he found himself incapable of proceeding with his literary labours of theological controversy and scriptural exegesis; and the language in which he described his admiration for what Rome had once been and his grief for the fate that has now overtaken her anticipates the language of Rutilius . . . the aggressively pagan *Praefectus Urbis emeritus*.

The shock administered by the fall of Rome in A.D. 410 to the citizens of a transient universal state which they had mistaken for an everlasting habitation has its counterpart in the shock suffered by the subjects of the Arab Caliphate when Bagdad fell to the Mongols in A.D. 1258. In the Roman world the shock was felt from Palestine to Gaul; in the Arab world, from Farghanah to Andalusia. 'It is difficult to estimate the bewilderment that Muslims felt. . . . Their suffering finds expression in the prayer offered in the great mosque of Bagdad on the Friday following the death of the Caliph: "Praise be to God who has caused exalted personages to perish and has given over to destruction the inhabitants of this city. . . . O God, help us in our misery, the like of which Islam and its children have never witnessed; we are God's and unto God do we return." ' " (Toynbee, *A Study of History*, VII, 11–12.)

"The intellectual wealth and the economic importance of this area (Transoceania) were extinguished for centuries to come" after the disruption of the Empire of Khwarazm-Shah caused by Mongols in

Western Imperialism

" What is the use of talking of Sargon, Harsha, and Napoleon, of Chinese, Turks, and Incas? They belong to the past which is dead and our concern is the present which is alive and furthermore totally different from the past. Tell us about the crimes of the British in India, the French in Algeria, the Americans in the Caribbean and Vietnam!" So speak those who are stylishly contemptuous of history and make of the part—Western imperialism—the whole, as if there had never been any other imperialism past or present. These are the same who ignore the common elements of human nature; the ties linking past, present and future; the limitedness of the range of aspirations giving direction to action, and of emotions regulating the speed of action; the slowness of the pace[32] at which change occurs at the most important level, which is that of institutions channelling relationships between people in a nation or any other independent community, and between nations.

The European Imperial Era

The modern era, the last four and a half centuries or so, is the European-American or Western era. Modern civiliza-

---

the 1220's. (B. Spuler, "The Disintegration of the Caliphate in the East," in Holt, Lambton, Lewis, eds., *The Cambridge History of Islam*, I, 162.)

32. There are "three different levels, at which history moves at different pace. . . . The level of personal action is the most superficial. At this level, history moves fastest, but the results are relatively ephemeral. At the institutional level the pace is slower; at the environmental level it is slower still." (Arnold Toynbee, "Illustrious Waters," in *World* (New York) of February 27, 1973, p. 44.) The institutional level is the one of interest in the discussion of wide-ranging developments.

tion has been in reality just the civilization of peoples inhabiting the western peninsula of the Eurasian landmass, and of their offshoots overseas. Beginning with the exploits of brave, ignorant, at times fanatically idealistic but more often plain greedy, and always cruel, Iberian adventurers five centuries ago, the modern era has been a European imperial era. Europeans left their homes and occupied and filled with their kin or with Africans violently uprooted in the most infamous commerce, the empty or near-empty quarters of the globe—in the Western Hemisphere, Australasia, Africa's southern tip. They established their control over, or subjected to their influence, the peoples of the populated quarters. The only nations to escape direct or indirect European rule were the few which adopted in time enough of Western ways to increase their strength to the point of being able to withstand the pressure of Europeans.

There was competition: from Ottoman and other Turks in the sixteenth and seventeenth centuries, from Eurasian Slavs conquering in all directions, from Chinese in the eighteenth century when they added millions of square miles to their vast ancient Empire, from Arabs reaching the interior of equatorial Africa in the nineteenth century, from Japanese in the western Pacific. Most competitors had to give way to the Europeans. In the historical scheme of modern times, the American nation—the most successful overseas offshoot of Europeans—participated in the European imperial drive, and in recent generations seemed well on the way to inheriting the imperial mantle.

The End of Western Imperialism

Not counting minor instances such as the ephemeral Swedish Empire or the imperial rule of Poles over non-Poles, both in the vast Polish Republic partitioned two centuries ago and in the smaller interwar Polish Republic, there have been in modern times more than twelve Western Empires or serious attempts at creating Empires. The same nation, the French for example, produced more than one imperial drive. Except for unimportant residues, Western imperialism is disappearing. In its wake it has left among the world intelligentsia a near-universal rejection of the Western way of life: not only the evils, defects and shortcomings but also what was good and valuable in it for the advancement of humanity.

Violence—not the violence of non-Westerners fighting Westerners, but of Westerners against each other in what are rightly called "fratricidal wars"[33]—has played a major role in ending the European-American era. Major, but not the only one. *The Battle of Algiers*, the film shown here in Wright Hall, documents the commitment of insurgents struggling against French rule: the insurgents would not have won without the active support of one-fourth of the French and the passive support of another fourth and more. A major—and unique—element in ending Western imperialism has been the rise and success of anti-imperialistic forces in Western imperial states endowed with free, democratic institutions.

Diversity Marks Western Civilization

Since the time when Greeks took up arms against the mighty Empire of the Persians there has been awareness of profound differences between the civilization of the West

33. "The violent breakdown of what was the European world order was brought on by the suicide of Europe in its fratricidal wars of 1914–1945 much more than by any irresistible revolt of the colonized peoples." (Herbert Lüthy, "Colonization and the Making of Mankind," in G. H. Nadel and P. Curtis, eds., *Imperialism and Colonialism* [New York: Macmillan, 1964], p. 35.)

and all other civilizations. In humankind's historical scheme Western civilization is the heresy; all other civilizations—from Pharaonic to fast-spreading national communism and national socialism—are the orthodoxy. It is orthodoxy to put as supreme good uniformity in what matters most, things of the spirit, and to accept coercion for the enforcement of uniformity. It is heresy to leave room for the citizens' autonomy and responsibility—to find place in society for some liberty.

Liberty breeds diversity. The diversity within the Western way of life is the antithesis of the uniformity elsewhere. Ancient Greece was deeply differentiated. So was medieval Europe. So has been the modern West. In "the . . . strange civilization of the West . . . a new world of universal ideas and material developments springing from them,"[34] in that strange civilization which fascinates and repels so many non-Westerners (and countless Westerners besides), it is distorting to lump different manifestations of imperialism together.

Western Conventional Imperialism

Much of Western imperialism has been of the conventional type already mentioned. Iberian imperialism, with which the modern European imperial era begins, did not deviate from the norm of imperial expansion: it was conquest by the state, imposition of the Iberian way of life, oppression of conquered peoples until such time as they ceased, through annihilation or assimilation, to exist; and creation meanwhile of hierarchical structures in which subjects were cut off from their past, lost their identity and at times their souls and the will to live. Spaniards, in the Americas, the Philip-

34. Spear, *India: A Modern History*, p. 105.

pines, their Mediterranean possessions, acted as the Chinese did in their closed continent and as Turks did in their several Empires. The Portuguese Empire, the French Napoleonic Empire, the attempted Italian Fascist Empire, and the German Nazi Empire were also conventional ones.

Western Heretical Imperialism

Different was the situation north of the Iberian peninsula, particularly among the English and all those who felt the influence of English ideas deeply, and who patterned, at least partially, their institutions on the English ones. One of the noblest and most generous British minds of the nineteenth century stated emphatically that "such a thing as the government of one people by another does not and cannot exist."[35] This was an exaggeration, because the government of one people by another has existed and still exists today, but millions of Britishers agreed that it should not. Writing on Western imperialism and referring specifically to the Anglo-Saxon brand, another author said: ". . . this must be the first time that an imperial power has come to examine its past acts upon subject peoples in the light of moral laws. . . ."[36]

35. John Stuart Mill, quoted in A. P. Thornton, *The Imperial Idea and Its Enemies* (London: Macmillan, 1963), p. iii.
36. "European imperialism does not differ so much from that of the past in its nature as in its consequences. . . . This must be the first time that an imperial power has come to examine its past acts upon subject peoples in the light of moral laws; for there is in the West a widespread and extraordinary desire to atone for the misdeeds committed as an imperial power. . . . We are beginning to assess the impact of nineteenth-century economic forces in mid-twentieth-century welfare terms, we are judging past actions by present standards. . . . This new guilt complex of the West . . . has helped to create and strengthen . . . the anticolonial movement of today." (Woodruff, *Impact of Western Man*, p. 58.)

Liberty and Anti-Imperialism

The development of anti-imperialism in an imperial nation seems strange. "Contradiction!" triumphantly shout upholders of the uniform conformist society. What is wrong with contradictions? They are the manifestation of what happens when people are to some extent free—free to think and to express themselves. Absolutism had triumphed in Iberia after the failure of the *comuneros*, and as generations went by it became ever more rigid. Some liberty had triumphed in Great Britain with the success of the Great Rebellion. Already centuries ago, Iberian nations and British nations and their offshoots in the Western Hemisphere were opposite poles in the variegated modern Western civilization: multiplicity of ideas and richness of life here, uniform conformity and barrenness of life there.

Liberty is not enough: fertile ground can produce poisonous weeds and fruitful trees. Liberty is the fertile ground of innovation but there is no guarantee that innovations will be born, or, if they are, that they will be good. There had been liberty but little or no conscious anti-imperialism in imperial Athens. There had been liberty but no widespread anti-imperialist movement in the republic of the United Provinces. In Great Britain there was, in the words of Gilbert Murray, the astounding phenomenon of "a privileged class giving up its privileges on grounds of conscience and humane principles."[37] Among the British the "antiimperialistic sentiment . . . begins with the moment when the struggle between the people and the crown ended . . .

37. Gilbert Murray, *From the League to the U.N.* (London: Oxford Univ. Press, 1948), p. 99.
"Ramsay MacDonald and Gilbert Murray insisted—and saw it as a matter for congratulation—that imperialism and democracy were incompatible." (Thornton, *The Imperial Idea*, p. 264.)

with the victory of the people,"[38] wrote a renowned Austrian-American economist. Since that "moment" (actually the period 1642–1688) the dynamism of enterprising citizens protected by a disciplined navy, whose freedom of action was increased by a fast-developing economy, favored imperial expansion. There was also sufficient liberty for anti-imperialistic Britishers to check abuses[39] and in time to assert themselves as a major force in the nation.[40]

From Empire to Commonwealth

Chatham delivered his last oration in support of Americans who no longer wanted to be British subjects. One hundred years ago Gladstone, the leader of the Liberal party, opposed the British imperialistic tide that was gathering new momentum,[41] and in 1959 a Conservative prime minister

38. "The defeat of the king and his party represent . . . a break in continuity. . . . By way of Charles I's scaffold, of Cromwell, of the Restoration, and of the events of 1688, the way led to freedom. . . ." (Schumpeter, *Imperialism*, p. 15.)

39. "We view the spirit in which the prosecution [of Negro rioters in Jamaica in 1865] has been treated by the nation generally, with sincere shame," wrote the Liberal weekly *Spectator* early in June 1868, supporting the Radicals' denunciation of the treatment of Jamaican blacks. (B. Semmel, *Democracy versus Empire: The Jamaica Riots of 1865 and the Governor Eyre Controversy* [New York: Doubleday, 1965], p. 181.)

40. "The other [school of opinion among us with respect to our Empire] . . . regards it as founded on aggression and rapacity, as useless and burdensome [and] advocates a policy which may lead at the earliest possible opportunity to the abandonment of it." (Sir J. R. Seeley, *The Expansion of England* [London: Macmillan, 1914; first printed in 1883], p. 341.)

41. "Wherever in the world a high aspiration was entertained, or a noble blow was struck, it was to England that the eyes of the oppressed were always turned— . . . where the people that had built up a noble edifice for themselves would, it was well known, be ready to do what in them lay to secure the benefit of the same inestimable

told his Soviet hosts in Moscow that the British would not hold on to their Empire.[42] Thanks to anti-imperialism at home there was a lessening of repression in British dependencies,[43] and those who were oppressed by colonial authorities could always successfully appeal to the bar of British opinion. The decision of the Imperial Conference held in London in 1926 to pursue the goal of equality of status[44] was implemented first through the participation of subject peoples in the administration of their countries,[45]

---

boon for others. You talk of the established policy and tradition. . . . I appeal to an established tradition, older, wiser, nobler far . . . which teaches . . . to seek the promotion of [British] interests in obeying the dictates of honour and justice." (W. E. Gladstone, speech of May 1877 [London: H.M.P.O., 3H234, May 7, 1877, 437–438].)

42. "We shall continue to grant independence as soon as the inhabitants of these territories are ready to exercise it." (Harold Macmillan in Moscow, quoted in *New York Times* of February 22, 1959.)

43. In British imperialism "cruelty played a lesser role between the two World Wars than ever before and a minimum of human rights was always safeguarded. It is this moderation . . . that paved the way for what Churchill has called 'the liquidation of His Majesty's Empire' and that eventually may turn out to mean the transformation of the English nation into a Commonwealth of English peoples." (Arendt, *The Origins of Totalitarianism*, p. 221.)

44. "Equality of status . . . is . . . the root principle governing our Inter-Imperial Relations." (Imperial Conference, 1926, *Summary of Proceedings* [London: H. M.'s Stationery Office, 1926], p. 15.)

45. "Indirect rule formed the basis of local government. . . . The African chief . . . appointed all officials who were responsible to him. He or his officials presided over the law courts which . . . applied African law. His agents levied taxes for the local treasury . . . for local improvement such as roads, sanitation, markets and schools. . . ." (Webster and Boahen, *History of West Africa*, p. 242.) In the case of British-controlled territories in India, Southeast Asia, the Middle East, Africa, indirect rule was not an intermediary stage between independence and annexation as had been (and is today) the case of conventional Empires but preparation for self-government, to be followed by independence.

then led to internal self-government and finally, from 1947 on, to the acceleration of the process which had started with Canada in 1867, transforming the Empire into a Commonwealth.[46] During the last half century fifteen former British dependencies and protectorates opted for independence outside the Commonwealth: no pressure was exercised to keep them in.

The Commonwealth is shaky; the hopes to which it had given rise have not been fulfilled; it is largely a name only and may soon not even be that. But the attempt was made to replace a vast imperial unit with an association enabling all members to have their own identity and to develop according to the free play of forces existing within the community. The Commonwealth represents a great advance over both imperialism and nationalism: it is failing, but at least it was tried.

Anti-Imperialism in Other Democracies

French imperialists were determined to hold on to their Empire—as recently as twenty years ago the third largest in the world—and to mould it into one uniform unit.[47] Their

46. "The colonies—of which Disraeli in 1852 had written: 'These wretched colonies . . . are a millstone round our necks' (Malmesbury, *Memoirs of an Ex-Minister*, p. 343)—these same colonies were to become autonomous members in a unified empire . . . crowned by a central representative organ in London, creating a closer, living connection between the imperial government and the colonies." (Schumpeter, *Imperialism*, p. 10.)

"Retirement from India was abdication of power. This, the imperialist view, was countered with the old Radical assertion, made by Attlee . . . and with due mention of Macaulay's name, that withdrawal of the British *Raj* was but the fulfilment of the British mission in India." (Thornton, *The Imperial Idea*, p. 328.)

47. "In December of 1934 . . . the first French Imperial Conference met. . . . The meeting had the purpose of preparing for the unity of *La France Totale*; of fusing into an economic imperial whole all the

134

efforts were frustrated by French anti-imperialists who sided with North African Muslims, with Indochinese, Malgache, and black African nationalists. A large section of the French nation helped insurgents during the Indochinese and Algerian wars, and more Frenchmen sympathized with the insurgents even if they did not give active help. The left-of-center half of the Dutch and Belgian[48] nations favored the independence of Indonesia and the Congo.

An Empire could have been created by the United States in the wake of the disruption caused by World War II.[49] Besides American military might and many plausible justifications—not all of them selfish or materialistic[50]—there was the desire of millions in European and western Pacific

---

inequalities, competitions, and variant economies of the motherland and her colonies." (H. I. Priestley, *France Overseas: A Study in Modern Imperialism* [New York: Appleton-Century, 1938], pp. 428–429.)

48. A former minister of colonies and leading member of the Belgian Liberal Party told me in Liège in 1958 that liberals and socialists —a majority of Belgians—were in favor of independence for the Congo.

49. "The strategic dominion of the United States . . . extends to 14,725,000 square miles outside our own borders and embraces a population of 667,815,000 'subjects.' " (George Marion, *Bases and Empire: A Chart of American Expansion* [New York: Fairplay Publishers, 1948], p. 168.) Bases never became dominion and there never were "subjects" as evidenced by the lack of an American reaction when the French government expelled American troops from France, and Pakistan not only dropped out of the "American" system of alliances but also joined hands with the opponent of the United States; as evidenced also by the disintegration of the "American" system of alliances in 1967–1973. Mr. Marion's book is a manifestation of the major factor in preventing the formation of an American Empire: the presence and influence of anti-imperialistic forces.

50. "The history of the Cold War shows that American foreign policy need not be the puppet of economic interests because much of it has not been." (M. Harrington, *Toward a Democratic Left* [New York: Macmillan, 1968], p. 216.)

nations, fearful of aggression, to be shielded by the United States. NATO was primarily the outcome of European initiative at a time when genuine anti-imperialists—socialist and other committed progressive democrats[51]—were a major force in European democracies. A vast system of alliances keyed to the United States was built between 1947 and 1955. The system of alliances could have become an Empire, as once happened with the Delian League, but, contrary to what Athens did with Naxos 2440 years ago, the United States, when member-states decided to drop out of the alliance to pursue neutral or even anti-American policies, did not prevent them from so doing.[52] Investments abroad compel the United States to kowtow to foreign governments threatening expropriation. The opposition of vast sections of the American public was the major factor in ending the Korean war with a military and political draw in 1953, and in ending the Vietnam war with a political defeat twenty years later. There could have been an American Empire; there is not. Because of internal divisions, and military weakness caused by the attitudes of majority sections of public opinion, there will not be an American Empire in the foreseeable future.

Events at the end of the century, when leadership will be

51. Influential political figures directly or indirectly involved in the negotiations leading to the North Atlantic Treaty of 1949 were in Great Britain Attlee and Bevin, in France Ramadier and Mayer, in Belgium Spaak, in the Netherlands Drees and Mansholt, in Denmark Hedtoft, in Norway Gerhardsen and Lange—all socialists. Deeply committed to democracy and anti-imperialism were the foreign ministers or prime ministers of Canada (Pearson), France (Schuman), Italy (Sforza) and Luxembourg (Bech).

52. "Our very existence . . . is an effective answer to the propaganda that the United States has aggressive designs." (Canadian Prime Minister Diefenbaker, quoted in L. L. Snyder, ed., *The Imperialism Reader* [Princeton: Van Nostrand, 1962], p. 601.)

136

in the hands of today's young, will show whether the American defeat and weakness have strengthened democracy and peace or—as I believe—dictatorship and aggression. This, however, is not the point: thanks to democratic liberties there is no American Empire, and as long as there is democracy there will not be one.

Democracy Checks Imperialism

Speaking to the Athenian assembly twenty-four hundred years ago, Cleon—leader of a party that now would be called progressive—said that "a democracy is incapable of empire...."[53] Cleon exaggerated: imperialistic drives exist in democracies, and when a democracy becomes strong it may impose its rule over weaker communities. But in a democracy there can happen what cannot happen when absolutism—dictatorial, monarchical, theocratic, oligarchic—is the rule: there can be the birth, growth and triumph of anti-imperialism. Among scores of Empires there have been imperial nations whose Empires collapsed because of the pressure of anti-imperialistic forces in the imperial nation itself: Athens was one and Great Britain has been another. There have been few nations in which imperial drives were checked by the pressure of anti-imperialistic forces: the United States is one. The dissolution of Iberian Empires in the Americas, initiated by the French occupation of Portugal and Spain, became final when the 1820 democratic revolutions in the two countries prevented the use of force in putting down insurgencies.

53. Cleon in 427 B.C., quoted in W. Lippmann, *Essays in the Public Philosophy* (Boston: Little, Brown, 1955), p. 45.

Two generations ago, the cumulative effect of defeats suffered by China in four minor wars and by Russia in one minor and one major war had temporarily ended the rule of Chinese and Russians over non-Chinese and non-Russians. Military defeats obliterated two German Empires, the overseas one in 1918 and the European one in 1945. Military defeats also obliterated what remained of the old Ottoman Empire in 1918 and the newer Italian and Japanese Empires in 1943 and 1945 respectively. Anti-imperialism in the imperial nation was the major factor in the collapse of four more European Empires—the British, the Dutch, the French, the Belgian—and in preventing the formation of an American Empire.

Even if only temporarily in some cases, two generations saw the collapse of twelve Empires in the twentieth century. Where only a few decades ago there had been a few vast Empires, there are now over eighty independent states, to which can be added dozens resulting from the earlier disintegration of the Iberian Empires in the Western Hemisphere, the Ottoman Empire before World War I, and the British Empire before World War II. "Anti-imperialism has won!" many say. One writer enthusiastically proclaimed a few years ago: "the phase of imperialism . . . is now nearing its end. . . . The trend . . . is irreversible."[54]

Not an Irreversible Trend

The trend is not irreversible. The fragmentation of the Macedonian Empire at the end of the fourth century B.C. facilitated the expansion of the Roman and the Parthian

54. S. C. Easton, *The Twilight of European Colonialism: A Political Analysis* (New York: Holt, Rinehart and Winston, 1960), p. 540.

Empires in the second. The fragmentation of the Mogul Empire during the first half of the eighteenth century facilitated the formation of the British Indian Empire during the second half, that of the Ottoman Empire stimulated (among others) Russian and British imperialism, facilitating Russian expansion in the north and British in the south of the former Ottoman domain.

Balkanization

Of the more than one hundred successor states of the European Empires and the Ottoman Empire, some have inner strength; most have none. There are vast areas—in the middle and southern sections of the Western Hemisphere, in Africa, the Middle East, southern and southeastern Asia— where the cohesion within independent states (few of which are nations) is weak, where tensions are strong, where cultural and economic levels are low. Low atmospheric pressure produces tornadoes, political weakness plays into the hands of the strong. It may not happen now, it may not happen for decades, but in much of the areas just mentioned present conditions are favorable to the rise of new Empires. Balkanization in central-south Europe favored German expansion in the thirties and Soviet expansion after Germany's military defeat. The process leading to the formation of new Empires may not be the same as that older process linked to the names of military and political geniuses, but the end result will be the same: the imposition of the rule of the strong over the weak, the killing, in the weaker nations, of creativity.

Restructuring of Two Empires

All Western Empires—except for the small Portuguese residue which will disintegrate when the revolution many are working at occurs in Portugal—have disappeared. In Western European nations and in the United States internal conditions make the renewal of imperial drives impossible. But two of the Empires disrupted early in this century have been restructured, and one of them has made considerable advances. One Empire includes nearly one-fourth of humankind, the other over one-sixth of the planet's land area; one is four times more populous than the United States, the other two and a half times its size.

China

One of the most influential nineteenth-century Russian revolutionaries[55] expressed concern one hundred years ago about the potential might of the Chinese nation, a concern now shared by the successors of other revolutionaries who restructured the Tsarist Empire as the Soviet Empire. The continuity of a superior civilization, commitment, intelligence, purposefulness, discipline and capacity for hard work, together with numbers entitle the Chinese to look at themselves as humankind's first nation. The fascination exerted by Maoist China[56] is great—greater than the combined fascination of Leninism and counter-Leninist Fascism in the twenties and thirties. The fascination is widespread among the dynamic minorities despotically ruling much of

55. "China . . . counts 400 million, or according to others 600 million inhabitants. . . . One does wrong to despise the Chinese masses. . . . Of late they have begun to familiarize themselves with modern arms and European discipline. . . . Just ally their discipline, the acquirement of new arms and modern tactics, with the primitive barbarism of the Chinese masses, with their total lack of any idea of human protest, of all instinct of liberty, with their habit of servile obedience . . . and you will understand how great is the peril. . . ." (N. Bakunin, quoted in Lichtheim, *Imperialism*, p. 96.)

56. "In Asia . . . the political left . . . is more likely to look north [to China] than across the Pacific for ideas." (S. R. Davis in "Asian Question Marks," *The Christian Science Monitor* of January 31, 1973.)

the Third World; it is an essential component of most of the New Left; it is increasing among the emotionally unstable sectors of the intelligentsia in democratic nations. Peoples included two hundred years ago in the Chinese Empire and now outside it number nearly one hundred and fifty millions: their countries are lost provinces to be joined one day to the imperial motherland.[57] When? Who knows? The fast expanding underground of fanatical terrorists existing in democracies and in the weak states of the Third World, and surfacing more and more, looks admiringly and expectantly at China[58] as millions of Europeans once looked at the United States. They look for help and for protection: China is the nation to which many of them already belong spiritually. They are the dynamic fifth column, doing for China what opponents of Moctezuma and Atahualpa once did for Cortez and Pizarro.

Soviet Union

The might of China is still potential, that of the Soviet Union, now the planet's strongest military power by far, is actual. From the Finns on the shores of frozen seas to Turks of steppes thousands of miles away, non-Russian peoples— half the population ruled by the Tsars—had broken away from the Russian Empire in 1917–1918. As in the course of a few seasons a Macedonian Empire replaced the Persian,

57. "The continued southward movement of the Han-Chinese . . . into . . . Southeastern Asia is inevitable." (Wiens, *China's March*, p. 348.)

58. "China . . . is stepping up every sort of activity in Africa: offering education, including that in guerrilla warfare; sending experts and entertainers; and diffusing a growing volume of influence by radio. . . . The Communists will direct against the old leaders the impatient young men as these return a few years hence from Marxist academies." (Margery Perkam, "The New Africa between East and West," in Nadel and Curtis, eds., *Imperialism and Colonialism*, p. 150.)

and a Mongol Empire replaced the Chinese, so in the course of a few seasons a Soviet Empire replaced the Tsarist one. Most peoples who had broken away were recaptured in 1920–1923, the others, except the Finns, in 1939–1940. Eight European and Asian peoples whom the Tsars had never conquered were absorbed in the Soviet imperial system in 1944–1948. In the revolutionary turmoil of 1917–1918 socialist internationalism was as much a victim as Tsarism. It was replaced by Soviet imperialism.[59] The wording changed, but Stalin's justification for Soviet imperial expansion was identical to the justification put forth by Tsarist spokemen.[60] The goals remained the same, but were pursued with greater efficiency.

59. "Soviet domination over the non-Russian peoples of the Soviet Union and over the satellite peoples of Europe and Asia is imperialism." (Hugh Seton-Watson, *The New Imperialism* [New York: Capricorn Books, 1961], p. 123.)

"After the autumn of 1956 . . . it is perfectly clear that Russia has pursued an imperialist policy in respect to her Eastern European dependencies. All the only too familiar circumstances of imperialism have been reproduced: . . . economic exploitation . . . resentment of the exploited peoples . . . rule by acquiescent 'puppet' governments . . . compromises with more or less nationalist governments . . . ruthless suppression of all opposition," wrote the former Stalinist, and influential Labour leader in Great Britain, Strachey (*The End of Empire*, pp. 296f.).

60. "The position of Russia in Central Asia is that . . . the more civilized state is forced, in the interest of the security of its frontier and its commercial relations, to exercise a certain ascendancy over those whom their turbulent and unsettled character make most undesirable neighbours." (Dispatch of 21 november / 3 december 1864, quoted in Bridges, Davies, Hargreaves, Scott, eds., *Nations and Empires; Documents in the History of Europe and Its Relations with the World since 1648* [London: Macmillan, 1969], p. 168.)

"Central Russia . . . cannot hold out long without the assistance of border regions, which abound in raw materials, fuel, and foodstuffs. The border regions of Russia . . . are inevitably doomed to imperialist bondage without the political, military, and organizational sup-

The Soviet society is not heretical, as the Athenian society once was and the American is today. It is an orthodox society, belonging to that mainstream of human life founded on monopoly of political power and on rigidly enforced conformism: there is neither room nor possibility for anti-imperialist forces to assert themselves.[61] Through annexations and the imposition of protectorates, one hundred and twenty million people were added a generation ago to Soviet manpower and military power. There are now—in Africa, the Western Hemisphere, south Asia, the Middle East—a score of states closely bound to the Soviet Union. Slow in taking decisions and quick in action, cautious and determined, the present Soviet leadership has increased the strength and prestige of the Soviet Union. It has had some setbacks, but the direction of the thrust remains forward. European imperialism has joined the imperialisms of the past, in the grave. American imperialism has not materialized. Soviet imperialism remains: favored by the Balkanization of much of the world resulting from the disintegra-

---

port of a more developed Central Russia. . . . The demand for the secession of the border regions from Russia . . . must be rejected . . . because it is fundamentally opposed to the interests of the mass of the peoples both of the center and of the border regions." (Joseph Stalin, *Marxism and the National and Colonial Question* [New York: Int. Publishers, n.d.], pp. 78–79.)

61. "Soviet society possesses no mysterious essence guaranteeing it from sin: on the contrary, the belief in its peculiar virtues is . . . an example of the sin of self-righteousness. . . . The interesting question presents itself, whether the evolution from self-righteousness to self-questioning, from the ruthless exercise of power to the abdication of the elite, which has taken place . . . in Britain and in France, will repeat itself in the Soviet Union. . . . There is not the slightest sign of the abdication of power by . . . the leadership of the Communist Party. The vigour and ruthlessness of the new imperialism still seem undiminished." (Seton-Watson, *The New Imperialism*, p. 128.)

143

tion of European Empires, it exerts relentless pressure against the enfeebled democracies.[62]

THE FUTURE

Law, the Alternative to Force

Should one conclude that there is nothing except "the general perspective of an age of revolutionary convulsions set off by imperialistic conflicts"[63]? Must humanity continue to witness the sordid struggle between the mighty who survive and the weak who are destroyed? Must there ultimately be no alternative for a nation other than "world domination or death"[64]? Of course not!—provided that force be replaced by law for the regulation of relations among nations.

There is imperialism because there is anarchy, and there is anarchy because there is sovereignty.[65] The end of sovereignty means the elimination of anarchy from the international scene. Imperialism will be checked. It will still raise its ugly head, just as within most societies cohesive groups try to replace law with their own arbitrary power, but it can be curbed, just as in a score or so of democracies citizens have learnt to repress the ambitions of ideological, economic and ethnic groups. Anarchy ends when rules which

62. "Much of the world is now divided between those who believe in the social and political doctrine of western liberal . . . democracy, and those who believe in its authoritarian opposite, Marxism-Leninism," centered in the Soviet Union (Woodruff, *Impact of Western Man*, p. 342).

63. Lichtheim, *Imperialism*, p. 12.

64. "Bernhardi's iterated watchword . . .—Weltmacht oder Niedergang— . . . is as if he said 'World-dominion or Death.' " (J. A. Cramb, *Germany and England* [London: Murray, 1914], p. 107.)

65. "Anarchy comes from the refusal . . . to renounce enough of . . . national sovereignty to let effective world law and order be set up." (C. K. Streit, *Union Now* [New York: Harper, 1949], p. 11.)

apply equally to all—to the mighty and to the weak, the literate and the illiterate, the well-born and the nameless orphan—and which are backed by an authority enforcing them (the rules called laws) replace absence of rules. This has been done within states and it has made for civilization. Hobbes notwithstanding,[66] it can be done among states and will make for a higher civilization.

The Hague, the League, the U.N.

There has been a beginning. Seventy-five years have gone by since a benevolent autocrat, who later paid with his life and that of his children for his benevolence, invited statesmen and jurists to a meeting to be held in the capital of the Netherlands. Twenty-six countries—over half the independent states of the time—sent their representatives to the First Hague Peace Conference. The immediate problem was the same that is discussed today in Helsinki, Vienna, Geneva: disarmament or at least limitation of armaments. The permanent problem was of course the replacement of force with law, and with organs capable of enforcing the law.[67] As to be expected, nothing conclusive was achieved then. Eight years later, at the suggestion of the American President, another meeting took place, and at the Second Hague Peace Conference the International Court of Arbitration (now the International Court of Justice) was born. It was not much, but the most difficult step in all initiatives, the first one, had been taken. Eleven years went by: in the midst of the thunder of thousands of guns and when mil-

66. "In the relations of independent nations . . . 'right and wrong, justice and injustice' have no place." (T. Hobbes, quoted in H. Sidgwick, *The Elements of Politics* [London: Macmillan, 1897], p. 240.)

67. "There ought to be an international police to enforce the judgements of international law." (Sir Oliver Lodge, *The War and After* [London: Methuen, 1915], p. 145.)

lions were dying from Flanders to the swamps of Iraq to save what little moral progress humankind had achieved, another American President announced the commitment of his Administration to the establishment of a League of Nations. The announcement was greeted with enthusiasm by many, with laughter by more.[68] The League came into existence in 1920: it was born handicapped, and within two decades had ceased to exist. It had nonetheless been a major step in the forward march of humankind.[69] Wilson's generous "view that the self-determination of nations, and national sovereignty, was a possible basis . . . of world peace"[70] had proved to be an illusion. But that the League failed is less important than the fact that it had existed—to be resurrected in 1945 as the United Nations through the commitment of two other great American Presidents.

Regional Organizations

There was a beginning. There is a continuation. The United Nations can do little to fulfil its main function—to maintain peace. Too many member-states want to achieve goals requiring the use of force. Too many people everywhere —including most self-styled pacifists—make the age-old distinction between just wars (their own) and unjust wars

68. "Our attitude is summed up in Lady Houston's thrilling 'Damn the League of Nations!' " (G. B. Shaw in article in *Time and Tide* for October 12, 1935.)

69. "The League of Nations steadfastly promoted international administration. . . . International, economic and social programs flowered in the fields of commerce, health, communications, and protection of helpless people. The Permanent Court . . . gained the respect of the world. . . . The League encouraged conferences and consultations. . . ." (C. J. Mangone, *A Short History of International Organization* [New York: McGraw-Hill, 1954], p. 153.)

70. A. Cobban, *The Nation State and National Self-Determination* (New York: Crowell, 1969), p. 64.

(those waged by others).[71] But at least a web of international institutions is being created through the activities of the fifteen agencies of the United Nations. It is a thin web of weak threads, but it is something—better than nothing.[72]

More important, in the shrinking world of democracies and minor authoritarian states linked to democracies and dependent on them, initiatives have been taken to create supra-national regional structures founded on agreement and not on force, respectful of the autonomy of its members. No regional structure has as yet eliminated the cancer of sovereignty among its members, but in some cases the cancer is being contained, and there is growing awareness that it must be controlled. OECD embraces twenty-three countries and functions. So does the eighteen-member Council of Europe. In the nine-member European Common Market the federal movement has many supporters. In the sixties several initiatives were taken to create integrated groupings of states in the western Pacific, the Caribbean, the Andean region. Nothing concrete has come from the initiatives yet but at least attempts have been made and are being made. Where there is no democracy, regional groupings either institutionalize imperialism (as in the case of the Mutual Assistance Council and its armed twin, the Warsaw Pact) or do not function.

71. "Not till the mind of man is filled with the conviction that . . . war . . . is a crime certain to be visited by condign punishment . . . will mankind be effectively rid of the menace." (H. A. L. Fisher, *A History of Europe from the Beginning of the 18th Century to 1937* [London: Spottswood, 1957], p. 1175.)

72. "The observer of international affairs can discern in the history of international organization a fascinating trend in world society. . . . International organizations have . . . multiplied. . . . International law . . . looks more and more toward treaty agreements rather than . . . custom." (Mangone, *A Short History of International Organization*, p. 10.)

147

World Federation vs. World Empire

Without claiming prophetic powers, with which no one is endowed, and simply extrapolating (with a question mark) from what has happened since paleolithic times, it is possible to argue that larger political units will one day replace smaller ones, that the existing situation is temporary—even if it continues for generations, even for centuries. Universal states have existed in sections of the planet once isolated or semi-isolated because of natural or artificial barriers—in the Indian sub-continent, the Chinese closed continent, the Andean mountain ranges, the Mexican highlands, the Mediterranean and Middle Eastern areas. A universal state may one day include all humankind. The process of unification can be a fast one. There were hundreds of sovereign states and independent tribal communities in the Mediterranean world in 367 B.C. when Romans began their imperial career, and in the Far Eastern "closed continent" in 247 B.C. when Shih Tuang-ti acceded to the throne of one of many kingdoms. By 146 B.C. Romans ruled the Mediterranean world, and by 108 B.C. the "closed continent" had one ruler.

When and if larger units come into existence on the planet—when and if a world state replaces the present twelve dozen or so sovereign states—it will make all the difference to the quality of life and to the future of humankind, whether they are the outcome of imperial expansion (in which case one culture will eliminate all others, uniformity will triumph and stagnation will set in), or whether they are the outcome of a contract freely concluded among nations agreed on limiting sovereignty and establishing a league, a confederation, a federation of self-governing,

148

autonomous units, each maintaining its identity, each capable of developing along its own chosen path.[73]

Open Road of Internationalism vs. Dead End of Imperialism

The Chinese Empire strangled the creativity of the peoples of China, of the conquerors as well as the conquered. It gave all a uniform culture, as stagnant—even if on a higher level—as the culture of ancient Egypt had been for thousands of years. The Roman Empire was well on the way to doing the same when, luckily for humanity, barbarians overran it and created conditions in which a new civilization would be born.

Advocates of European unity were committed opponents of Hitler, whose armies nearly created a united Europe; they are weary today of Soviet blandishments promising the taking down of the curtain raised in 1944–1961, and the formation of a united Europe. Why the opposition, why the weariness? Because these advocates of unity reject the dead end of despotism and want the open road of democracy; because they reject the stagnation implicit in the long or short run in twentieth-century totalitarianism and want progress; because the unity of the free opens the road to a better future while the unity of the unfree leads to the grave; because they do not want the triumph of a nation but the integration of humankind differentiated in hundreds of nations; because, paraphrasing Hegel, they agree that

73. "Before the end of the present century, unless something quite unforeseeable occurs, one of three possibilities will have been realized . . . : The end of human life. . . . A reversion to barbarism. . . . A unification of the world . . . by the victory of the United States in the next world war, or by the victory of the U.S.S.R., or . . . by agreement . . . [among] nations that desire an international government. . . ." (B. Russell, "The Future of Mankind," in W. F. Irmscher, *Man and Warfare* [Boston: Little, Brown, 1964], pp. 145–147.)

"above and beyond the nation-state there is the spirit of humankind."[74]

Internationalism Is Bound to Democracy

To establish an imperial order and keep it going requires only force. A democratic international order raises the problems faced by those who in the past replaced absolutism with the heresy of liberty. Which are the laws that are not tyrannical, that emancipate citizens while satisfying the requirements of organized society and of the social order? Who is going to make the laws? What is the procedure for making them? Who is going to enforce them, and how?

The answer to these questions is to be found in the Covenant of the League of Nations and in the Charter of the United Nations. Both Covenant and Charter were the projection onto the international scene of the institutions through which liberty had been organized, and which had created modern democracy. They were the projection of the ideas, values and aspirations underlying these institutions. Democracy and internationalism are indivisible. The success of the League and the U.N. required the diffusion and consolidation of democracy. Instead, democracy shrank and weakened, in the thirties and now again: the League failed and the U.N. survives by functioning as little as possible.

Dictatorship Fathers Imperialism

Supported by force, absolutism and Empire need only minimal consent. Democracy cannot survive long unless consent is widely diffused among citizens; and a league of states, founded on the principle that the rule of law replaces

74. Quoted in Sir Oliver Lodge, *The War and After*, p. 7.

force, cannot function unless a majority of its members have democratic institutions. Each dictatorship established in the twenties and thirties in member-states—in Italy in 1922, in Brazil in 1930, in Japan in 1932, in Germany in 1933—was a nail crucifying the League. Each dictatorship established in member-states crucifies the United Nations. With the advent of dictatorships in most African[75] and other newly independent countries, authoritarian states now form nearly three-fourths of the U.N. membership. Regimes founded internally on force see in force the instrument for the solution of external conflicts. Contempt for the rule of law internally means contempt for law internationally, means that force remains the arbiter in international relations.

Each plaudit for a dictatorship is a blow to the cause of international cooperation as alternative to imperialism, in the age-old process of humankind's integration.[76] It weakens efforts to create an international order founded on law, strengthens international anarchy, is a vote for imperialism. The struggle for an international order of nations "free and equal" cannot be divorced from the struggle for internal democracy in all nations. Liberty *must* precede union if the road to progress is to remain open.

75. "Few African nations have retained the multi-party system with which most of them entered independence. Opposition is . . . tolerated only in a few, and even in these it may soon disappear. The governing party will perpetuate itself and rule as it wishes until a revolution or rebellion overthrows it; or perhaps the army will replace it. . . ." (Stewart C. Easton, *The Rise and Fall of Western Colonialism: A Historical Survey from the Early Nineteenth Century* [New York: Praeger, 1964], p. viii.)

76. "From the earliest dawn of history . . . down to the present day, the tendency to form continually larger political societies . . . seems to accompany the growth of civilization." (Sidgwick, *The Elements of Politics*, p. 218.)

Must refers to the ethical imperative, not to what will happen—to duty, not to success. "But what am I, what can I do?" is the despairing cry arising from millions painfully aware of their own infinitesimal smallness. Of course, the political responsibility of each, the contribution each makes to the tragedy called history is for the overwhelming majority so microscopic as to seem non-existent. Not so with moral responsibility, which is all-important and is equal for all, whatever the station in life, the capacity, the intellect, the position, the authority. Morally, we all share in what happens, we are all participants in the events. Therefore, each needs to know where he or she stands.

In terms of the theme of this Alumnae College, the choice is between democracy and the creation of an international order founded on law on one side, dictatorship and imperialism on the other. Those who stand for democracy and a meaningful United Nations Organization are a dwindling minority. Discouragement is easy. There is no discouragement if one heeds the French Huguenots' "point n'est besoin d'espoir pour entreprendre ni de succès pour persévérer," or as a great human being, Alan Paton, wrote not long ago: "When one strives to achieve a just order, one does not do it in order to be successful, one does it because that is what one must do."[77] The just order is not the Empire—any Empire: it is the association of nations subject to laws, freely enacted and equal for all.

Max Salvadori

77. Alan Paton, "White South Africa's Only Hope of Survival," in *The New York Times Magazine* of May 13, 1973, p. 39.

SMITH COLLEGE STUDIES IN HISTORY

The SMITH COLLEGE STUDIES IN HISTORY, begun in 1915 under the editorship of Sidney B. Fay, has published to date something over sixty books and monographs in various fields of history. The range of subjects has been intentionally wide, including the fields of American and European history, and stretching in time from the Ancient world to the present. The STUDIES has published monographic research as well as critical editions in translation of significant historical documents. Orders for copies or requests for exchange should be addressed to: Order Department, Smith College Library, Northampton, Massachusetts 01060.

157

Deyrup, Felicia J. *Arms Makers of the Connecticut Valley: A Regional Study of the Economic Development of the Small Arms Industry, 1798–1870.* 1948. (Out of print) Available: Univ. Microfilms, Inc. O. P. #25277

VOLUME XXXIV

Bornholdt, Laura. *Baltimore and Early Pan-Americanism.* 1949.

VOLUME XXXV

Gragg, Florence A., and Gabel, Leona C. *The Commentaries of Pius II.* Bks. VI–IX. 1951.

VOLUME XXXVI

Bourland, Caroline B. *The Guild of St. Ambrose or Schoolmasters' Guild of Antwerp 1529–1579.* 1951.

VOLUME XXXVII

Hutner, Frances Cornwall. *The Farr Alpaca Company. A Case Study in Business History.* 1951.

VOLUME XXXVIII

Gordon, Cyrus H. *Smith College Tablets. 110 Cuneiform Texts Selected from the College Collection.* 1952.

VOLUME XXXIX

Geyl, Pieter. *From Ranke to Toynbee.* 1952.

VOLUME XL

Hecht, Jean. *Continental and Colonial Servants in 18th Century England. 1954.*

VOLUME XLI

Taber, Martha V. H. *A History of the Cutlery Industry in the Connecticut Valley.* 1955.

VOLUME XLII

Cohn-Haft, Louis. *The Public Physicians of Ancient Greece.* 1956.

VOLUME XLIII

Gragg, Florence A., and Gabel, Leona C. *The Commentaries of Pius II.* Bks. X–XIII. 1957.

VOLUME XLIV

Gabel, Leona C., *et al. The Renaissance Reconsidered: A Symposium.* 1964.

VOLUME XLV

Lehmann, Phyllis W., *et al. A Land Called Crete; A Symposium in Memory of Harriet Boyd Hawes, 1871–1945.* 1967. $5.75.

VOLUME XLVI

Pevsner, Nikolaus. *Robert Willis.* 1970. $2.50.

PRINTED AT
THE STINEHOUR PRESS